The Time of the End

The 10 Year Tribulation Period
and
The Conditional Rapture of Tribulation Saints

The Time of the End

The 10 Year Tribulation Period
and
The Conditional Rapture of Tribulation Saints

Matthew S. Crane, B.D.

First Edition: November 2017

Printed in the United States of America
ISBN: 9781719801096

The lips of the wise disperse knowledge: but the heart of the foolish doeth not so.
Proverbs 15:7

Table of Contents

A Note to the Reader

I am a King James Bible <u>believer</u>. But more than simply that, I am a King James Bible <u>reader</u> and a King James Bible <u>studier</u>. I graduated from Pensacola Bible Institute in 2011, and cannot describe how grateful I am to the Lord for giving me the opportunity to learn under Dr. Peter S. Ruckman and Pastor Brian Donovan. While I was there, I took to heart my teachers' admonition of studying the Bible for myself and having it as my final authority.

The following thesis and the new concepts contained herein are the result of years of study on this subject. Perhaps this new material has already been written; if so, I have never come across it, and the new concepts that I discuss in this thesis, namely (1) the length of the entire "Tribulation period" and (2) the conditional rapture of Jewish "Tribulation" saints are the results of my own studies and are original.

The reader will find a lot of material in this thesis that will not line up with the standard, commonly accepted teachings on the subject of the Tribulation period. I want to emphasize that <u>honest DISAGREEMENT doe not equal DISRESPECT</u>. To suggest otherwise is a sure marking of a CULT mentality. It does not matter who the teacher is, what their level of education is, or what their accomplishments are; when it comes to the Bible, if a proposed theory is found out to be inconsistent, it needs to be changed because it must be <u>wrong</u>, for God's word is not inconsistent. To suggest otherwise is a sure marking of a C-U-L-T mentality that puts loyalty to men's brains above loyalty to God's words.

Furthermore, <u>honest DISAGREEMENT doe not equal PRIDE.</u> If a teaching is wrong, someone needs to say "that is wrong". This is not pride, but is simply the uncomfortable chafing of truth and fact.

Do not get mad yet, we have not even started; just THINK about these things for a while, and do as the Bible commands YOU to do: **"Prove all things; hold fast that which is good"**.[1]

---

[1] 1 Thessalonians 5:21

2

Introduction

I would like to propose a couple of theories that would explain a number of Bible passages that still, to this day, are ambiguous at best.

As a disclaimer, I will not take up the reader's time with arguments based on a single verse or verses wrested out of context, nor will I belabor over teachings that have already been thoroughly exhausted. However, due to the nature of the book of Revelation and Bible prophecy, it is impossible to isolate a singular eschatological subject without briefly taking into consideration other aspects of prophecy, for all prophetic events correlate in some way with other prophetic events. In this thesis, I will take for granted that the reader subscribes to a literal interpretation of the Scriptures and has an understanding of eschatology from a dispensational, Pre-Millennial, Pre-Tribulation rapture standpoint, and will attempt to focus on the subject matter rather than write an entire commentary on the book of Revelation.

Most of the Scripture references in this book are printed out in the footnotes. This makes this thesis seem longer than it really is, but I mention this for two reasons: 1) To encourage the reader to read the book in its entirety, and 2) To let the reader see the verses for himself, so he can properly judge the subject matter according to the word of God. To simply list all of the references would make for a shorter book, but would not help with facilitating discernment as to whether what I am presenting is Scriptural or not, for there are so many verses to back up these theories that if the reader had to look up each one for himself, he would probably never finish reading the thesis. Most of the Scripture references are emboldened to distinguish the verses from the rest of the common text

- - - - - - - - - - - - -

Over the last 2,000 years, various doctrines have been hashed out by the body of Christ; the Trinity, the deity of Christ, eternal security, the free will of man, the sovereignty of God, a-millennialism, post-millennialism, and many other theological subjects have been hammered out on the anvil of the word of God, and so naturally, the final argument came down to the authority of the Bible itself and whether or not we currently possess the perfect SCRIPTURES; or, have they been lost in antiquity and all that remains is "reliable" copies of copies? However, now even the Bible version issue seems to be an exhausted subject. What further evidence would need to be presented to show that the King James Bible is superior to any and all other new Bible versions? Furthermore, what further evidence would need to be presented to prove that the King James Bible is superior to the "original" manuscripts?!

Since the FINAL ISSUE is FINAL AUTHORITY, and since this issue has already been resolved by anyone interested in finding the truth, it would seem that the Church Age should be complete and we born again Christians should have been out of here by now. It seems as though we are now in "overtime", and in these last days an old argument is beginning to revive. This argument has always been in the background, but has never been brought to the forefront of Christian debate like it is now. The debate among the body of Christ these days has to do with the events of the "Tribulation period" (as it is commonly referred to), the Church's presence or absence during that time, and the timing of the rapture.

This is not a superfluous subject; to the contrary, it is entirely appropriate for a longing bride to be interested in the coming of her spouse, and yet a growing number of Christians are becoming anxious and beginning to wonder if Jesus is indeed coming to get them, or if they are destined to go through the Tribulation period. Many today are teaching that the Church is destined to go through the Tribulation period and that the doctrine of the imminent return of Jesus Christ - i.e. "The rapture" - is nothing more than the heretical ramblings of a demon possessed Charismatic girl from the 1800s.

This non-sense about the Church having to go through

4

"JACOB'S TROUBLE"[2] has been around for a very long time, but what makes the situation different this time is that these things are now being taught by men who

1. USED to believe in a Pre-Tribulation rapture
2. Are conservative patriots
3. Are King James Bible Believin', Street-Preachin', Hell-blastin', etc....

These three things create "the perfect storm" when it comes to subverting Laodicean Christians who barely read (and certainly do not study) their Bibles.

This heresy, I believe, is in a large part a result of "pre-tribbers" being a little too loose with the Scriptures that they use to PROVE a pre-tribulation rapture. A pre-tribulation rapture of the Church is certainly found in the word of God, but the ever present danger is taking a verse out of context to prove and support a legitimate teaching elsewhere in the Bible. This is a very common practice among Christians who believe in salvation by grace through faith, which is a legitimate doctrine, but then try to cram their New Testament / Church Age theology into Old Testament passages. This same folly has happened with Pre-Tribulation theology. For example:

Mark 13:32 But of that day and *that* hour knoweth no man, no, not the angels which are in heaven, neither the Son, but the Father....

v.35 Watch ye therefore: for ye know not when the master of the house cometh, at even, or at midnight, or at the cockcrowing, or in the morning:

This text has been used over and over to teach that the rapture of the Church is imminent, that any attempt at "date setting" is a violation of the words of Christ, and that everyone needs to be watching for the rapture because it can happen at any time. Even if some or all of those things are true, THIS SPECIFIC TEXT CANNOT BE USED AS PROOF FOR ANY OF THOSE ARGUMENTS! Any application to the Church from **Mark 13:32-35** is wresting the verses out of their context, and "a text without a

---

[2] **Jeremiah 30:7 Alas! for that day *is* great, so that none *is* like it: it *is* even the time of Jacob's trouble; but he shall be saved out of it.**

5

context is a PRETEXT", even if the teacher is an independent King James Bible Believing Baptist. The context is **"THAT DAY"** and **"THAT DAY"** is NOT a reference to the rapture of the Church but rather an event that occurs during the Tribulation period.

Here is another good one:
Luke 12:37 Blessed *are* those servants, whom the lord when he cometh shall find watching: verily I say unto you, that he shall gird himself, and make them to sit down to meat, and will come forth and serve them.
Again, how this text can possibly be applied to a Church Age rapture is past finding out. The context is the Lord returning <u>FROM</u> a wedding[3]!! If He is coming to GET his bride, but returning FROM a wedding, WHO DID HE MARRY?!
You see, these verses present a problem that hitherto has been solved by:
1. Correcting the Bible text, i.e. changing the verse to fit your theology, or
2. Ignoring the context, i.e. you stubbornly cram your theology (in this case, Pre-Tribulation rapture theology) into the text like any good Mormon, Catholic, or Jehovah's Witness.

A growing number of astute Christians have picked up on this kind of lackadaisical exposition and have noticed the gaping doctrinal HOLES that appear when these verses are applied to a Pre-Tribulation rapture; so in despair and/or frustration, they have abandoned their 'pre-trib' position and succumbed to a 'post-trib' position. After all, the above texts are apparently talking about a rapture of <u>living</u> saints, and the above texts (and others like it in Matthew, Mark and Luke) have a Tribulation / 2nd Advent context, therefore they conclude that "the church must be raptured sometime <u>during</u> the Tribulation period."
In a way, these "post-trib / mid-trib Frankensteins" are monsters of our (Bible Believer's) own making. By twisting the contexts in

---

[3] **Luke 12:36 And ye yourselves like unto men that wait for their lord, when he will return FROM THE WEDDING; that when he cometh and knocketh, they may open unto him immediately.**

6

the Gospels to support the Pre-Tribulation rapture of the Church, the natural result was for an Absalom to come along, see the hypocrisy of the situation and then win the people's hearts through YouTube and Facebook and wreak havoc on SOUND Pre-Tribulation rapture DOCTRINE by teaching that the way you reconcile these apparent contradictions is by conceding that the rapture of the Church must occur sometime during the Tribulation period.

This problem has persisted long enough that the Body of Christ has been splintered even further into various groups: some are "pre-tribbers", some are "mid-tribbers", some are "post-trib / pre-wrath-ers", some are "post-tribbers" and most do not even care.

Why is there so much debate on this subject? Is the Bible really that vague? Of course not. The problem is never with the Bible but rather our feeble understanding of the Bible. Centuries ago, the body of Christ debated vehemently over Calvinism vs. Armenianism. A subject that seemed biblically vague to them at that time is now crystal clear to us today. In the same way, there is a DEFINITE, CLEAR answer to this 'post-trib' vs. 'pre-trib' debate, it just is not clear YET, and even though the answer of *"I am not to going to be there so I don't care"* might sound cute, it is nothing more than an admission of laziness, disrespect for the word of God, and lack of concern for the Lord's sheep. The fact of the matter is, Tribulation teaching is not just a mental rubix cube for heady theologians to argue and waste time over. One's position on this subject has very practical implications. After all, if the Tribulation is coming, we had better stockpile food and ammo and oppose the Antichrist's NWO[4] by opposing our government! If we are going to go through the Tribulation, then we need to be warning Christians about taking the mark of the Beast – oh but wait, can a Christian who is sealed by the Holy Spirit lose his salvation?! .....Oh I KNOW: A person who takes the mark of the Beast was never TRULY saved to begin with...blah...blah...blah.

The timing of the rapture and whether or not the Church goes through the Tribulation period has practical ramifications in the lives of God's people, so these doctrines need to be understood. It

---

[4] New World Order

is the job of all Christians to study[5] (especially the pastors!) and failure to do so is not only shameful[6], but it is sinful. The Lord absolutely has all of the answers in his word, and even though the body of Christ will certainly NOT BE PRESENT for ANY PART of the Tribulation period, the Lord is evidently allowing the Body of Christ to hash these subjects out so as to give his chosen people (the Jews) a theological head start....because they are going to need all of the help that they can get.

---

[5] 2 Timothy 2:15 STUDY to shew thyself approved unto God.....
[6] 2 Timothy 2:15 ....a workman that needeth not to be ASHAMED, rightly dividing the word of truth.

Chapter 1

Terminology and Definitions

When it comes to the study of eschatology, there are many different theories and thoughts circulating as to how the book of Revelation plays out. This is the second edition of this thesis, and based upon feedback that I received from the first edition, I realized that there is a great need of consistency in terminology as it relates to these subjects. For example: if I said, *"the Church is going to be raptured out before the Tribulation period begins"*, that could mean a lot of different things depending on your understanding of the Tribulation period. To one person, "Tribulation" refers to a 7 year time period, divided into two equal parts of 3 ½ years; to another, "Tribulation" might mean a 3 ½ year time period, and so on. This confusion of vocabulary was a problem in the first edition, so I will here define some words and terminology as they will be used throughout the rest of this thesis.

1. Tribulation

This is a general word that can refer to "severe affliction; distresses of life; vexations; often denotes the troubles and distresses which proceed from persecution."[7] "Tribulation" does NOT always refer to the future apocalyptic time period described in the book of Revelation as evidenced by the following verses:

2 Corinthians 7:4 Great *is* my boldness of speech toward you, great *is* my glorying of you: I am filled with comfort, I am exceeding joyful in all our tribulation.

Paul was not experiencing the "Tribulation period", he was simply experiencing "tribulation" (severe affliction).

1 Thessalonians 3:4 For verily, when we were with you, we told you before that we should suffer tribulation; even as it came to pass, and ye know.

According to this passage, if "tribulation" always referred to the

---

[7] Webster's 1828 Dictionary

events described in the book of Revelation, then the Thessalonians already endured the "Tribulation period" and it is now OVER!

"Tribulation" often has nothing to do with a specific time period; nevertheless, we should be careful to observe that sometimes the word can have a dual application:

John 16:33 These things I have spoken unto you, that in me ye might have peace. In the world ye shall have tribulation: but be of good cheer; I have overcome the world.

This can apply to general tribulation (severe afflictions) or we could legitimately make application to the coming Tribulation period, which will obviously occur **"in the world"**.

2 Thessalonians 1:6 Seeing *it is* a righteous thing with God to recompense tribulation to them that trouble you;

In this context, "tribulation" is used in its general sense; however the Lord will certainly punish the world by means of the coming "Tribulation period", so it can be applied both ways.

As can be clearly seen, the word "tribulation" can be an ambiguous word that has to be interpreted according to its context. For this reason, I will try to avoid using the term "tribulation" and instead rely on more specific verbiage to describe the time period spoken of in the book of Revelation.

2. Satan's Advent

This exact term, of course, is not found in the Bible, but it is descriptive of a specific, key event in the Scriptures. I will frequently use this term to refer to the moment when the Antichrist stands in the Holy Place / rises from the dead. Technically, these two events will (probably) be separated by 3 days (as a counterfeit of Jesus Christ's death, burial and resurrection); nevertheless, this prophetic milestone called "Satan's Advent" is the Devil's manifestation in the flesh and the commencement of the final 3 ½ years of Daniel's 70th week.

3. The Great Tribulation

This is much more specific than "tribulation". Paul never refers to his sufferings and afflictions as "great tribulation". This is a term that Jesus used to describe the apocalyptic events that will occur AFTER the Church is raptured and AFTER the man of sin stands in the Holy Place.

Matthew 24:21 For THEN shall be great tribulation, such as was not since the beginning of the world to this time, no, nor ever shall be.

When does the **"then"** refer to? It refers back to the event of verse 15: **When ye therefore shall see the abomination of desolation, spoken of by Daniel the prophet, stand in the holy place,** [i.e. Satan's Advent]**(whoso readeth, let him understand:) v.16 THEN let them which be in Judaea flee into the mountains....**

v.21 For THEN shall be <u>great tribulation</u>**....**

The specific application of the term **"great tribulation"** is important to understand: if there is a time gap between the rapture of the Church and the appearance of the man of sin in the Holy Place, then it is critical to note that this interim time cannot be called the **"great tribulation"**, for the **"great tribulation"** can ONLY refer to the time period that begins with Satan's Advent (the man of sin standing in the Holy place) and ends with the 2nd Advent of Jesus Christ.

I should also point out that the <u>final 3 ½ year time period</u> known as the **"great tribulation"** is also called **"the end"** in **Matthew 24:6, 24:14, Daniel 9:26, 11:35** and **Mark 13:7**. It is also called **"the time of Jacob's Trouble"** in **Jeremiah 30:7**. To avoid confusion, I will <u>only</u> use the term **"great tribulation"** to refer to the final 3 ½ years of Daniel's 70th week.

4. The Beginning of Sorrows

Matthew 24:6 And ye shall hear of wars and rumours of wars: see that ye be not troubled: for all *these things* **must come to pass, <u>but the end is not yet.</u>**
v.7 For nation shall rise against nation, and kingdom against kingdom: and there shall be famines, and pestilences, and

earthquakes, in divers places.
v.8 All these *are* the beginning of sorrows.

If we were to take the typical 7 year tribulation teaching, we would argue that the first 3 ½ years is "(general) tribulation" and the last 3 ½ years is "great tribulation". This type of labeling can become very ambiguous very quickly, so I will use the terminology that Jesus used to describe these two separate time periods: the time from the rapture of the Church to Satan's Advent I will refer to as **"the beginning of sorrows"** and the time from the Satan's Advent to the 2nd Advent of Jesus Christ I will refer to as the **"Great Tribulation [period]"**.

5. The Time of the End (or End Times)

This is a phrase that is used in **Daniel 8:17, 11:35, 11:40, 12:4** and **12:9** and is more comprehensive in that it can not only refer to the final 3 ½ years (great tribulation period) but <u>also</u> the time period that precedes it (the beginning of sorrows). In this thesis I will exclusively use the term "the Time of the End" or "End Times" to refer <u>to the ENTIRE LENGTH of time from the rapture of the Church to the 2nd Advent.</u> The usage of these five terms as they pertain to the prophetic events described in the book of Revelation is shown on Chart 1 on page 13:

CHART 1

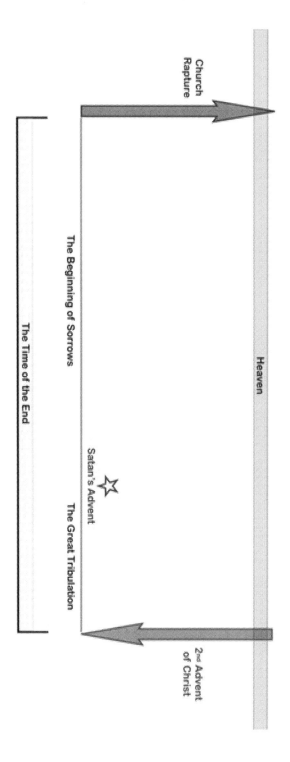

Church Rapture

Heaven

The Beginning of Sorrows

Satan's Advent

The Great Tribulation

The Time of the End

2nd Advent of Christ

CHAPTER 2

THE COMING RAPTURE<u>S</u>

The word "rapture" is word that is not found anywhere in the Bible. The actual Bible word is **"translated"**[8], however for the sake of understanding, I will stick with the word "rapture" to describe the phenomenon of a person or persons being BODILY caught up INTO THE AIR and taken into HEAVEN.

It has long been taught that there are two raptures yet to occur: the first rapture is the rapture of the Church which is exclusive to born again Christians who can be dead or alive, and this rapture occurs BEFORE the Time of the End begins.[9] The second rapture is considered to be toward the very END of the Great Tribulation period and involves the bodily ascension of <u>dead</u> tribulation saints.[10]

In this thesis, I will propose a theory that will provide an answer to much of the perceived ambiguity regarding the timing of the Church's rapture: whether it will be before, in the middle of, or at the end of the Great Tribulation period. This theory will also impart a solution to many of the difficult "rapture" passages contained in the Gospels that are often misapplied to the rapture of the Church.

If this theory is incorrect, then it belongs in the wastebasket with all of the other nonsense such as Harold Camping's rapture / Judgment Day strike out and Steven Anderson's "After the Tribulation" delusional ramblings. I have personally scrutinized this theory for nearly a decade only to find that it fits the "prophecy puzzle" better and better the more I study it out. I invite everyone who reads this thesis (in its ENTIRITY) to punch holes in it IF you can.

I propose that there is another rapture; a THIRD rapture.

---

[8] **Hebrews 11:5 By faith Enoch was translated that he should not see death; and was not found, because God had translated him: for before his translation he had this testimony, that he pleased God.**
[9] **1 Thessalonians 4:13-18; 1 Cor. 15:51-55; Song of Solomon 2:10-13; Genesis 5:24**
[10] **Revelation 11:7-12, 14:14-16**

Before I explain what and when and why and how, allow me to first ask the reader a question: *Why is it that so many Christians believe in a "mid-tribulation" rapture?* Why is it that so many Christians think that the rapture is conditional upon individual behavior or faithfulness? If there were clearly zero Scriptural evidences to support such claims, these teachings would not have gained so much traction among God's people. Dr. Peter S. Ruckman has often said, "Every heresy in this age is a doctrinal truth belonging to a different dispensation." In other words, heresies would not be so prevalent if there were no Scripture verses to back them up; but there ARE verses to back them up, and sometimes a LOT of verses. However, failure to RIGHTLY DIVIDE the Scriptures is almost always the origin of these false teachings. What is true for one group of people during a certain time may not be true for another group of people at a different time. Without a "dispensational" understanding of the Bible, countless doctrines get scrambled together, and once the "dispensational boundaries" have been removed, the bread of God's word becomes a "soup sandwich" (to quote Dr. David Peacock).

I believe a similar mix-up has occurred in regard to the idea of a mid-tribulation rapture. Indeed there IS going to be a "mid-tribulation rapture" but it has NOTHING TO DO WITH THE CHURCH / BODY OF CHRIST.

There are three future raptures and they are as follows:
The FIRST rapture is the rapture of the Church and precedes the Time of the End. It is exclusive to born again Christians, and it does not matter whether they are dead or alive at that time.

The SECOND rapture is a rapture of LIVING Jewish saints which will occur sometime around the middle of the Time of the End. The thing that is significant about this rapture is there is a CONDITION attached to it, which will be explained later.

The THIRD rapture is a rapture of DEAD saints which will occur toward the very end of the Great Tribulation period.

CHAPTER 3

The Rapture Types in the Bible

There are THREE men in the Bible that were "raptured" into heaven; that is, their BODIES were taken up INTO THE AIR and did not come back[11]: Enoch, Moses, and Elijah.

1. Enoch

Enoch's rapture is a type of the rapture of the Church. This is evidenced by the fact that Enoch is in many ways similar to a Church Age Christian in that he lived before the Law, his righteousness was based upon his relationship with God, he was neither Jew nor Gentile[12], and he was taken out <u>before</u> the flood (type of the Great Tribulation). Notice that Enoch was not raptured mid-way through the flood or after the flood; he was raptured BEFORE the flood!

2. Moses

I am skipping the prophetic chronological order here, but Moses is a type of the <u>dead</u> tribulation saint that goes up sometime toward the end of the Great Tribulation period.

Moses' salvation was contingent upon faith and works, just as salvation will be for people who are alive during the End Times. Moses died and was buried in a valley somewhere in Moab[13], and shortly after his death an ANGEL came along to take his BODY up to heaven[14]. This was not just any angel, this was Michael the

---

[11] Philip's strange experience in **Acts 9:39-40** is technically not a "rapture" since his body was set back down in Azotus. Ezekiel also was not "raptured" in **Ezekiel 8:3** because his transportation only involved his spirit and not his body.

[12] The Jewish people were not called out and chosen by God until the time of Abram which was many years after Enoch and the Flood.

[13] **Deuteronomy 34:5-6**

[14] **Revelation 14:15 And another <u>angel</u> came out of the temple, crying with a loud voice to him that sat on the cloud, Thrust in thy sickle, and reap: for the time is come for thee to reap; for the harvest of the earth is ripe.**
v.16 And he that sat on the cloud thrust in his sickle on the earth; and the earth was reaped.

Archangel[15], a character who is directly associated with the Time of the End according to **Revelation 12**[16] and **Daniel 12**[17]. Furthermore, at the time when Moses' body was taken up, Satan was standing nearby ON THE GROUND[18]. These details match the details given in **Revelation 11** in which the two witnesses are caught up into heaven presumably along with all of the other dead tribulation saints.[19]

3. Elijah

This is where things get interesting. Most Bible Believers are familiar with the rapture types found in Enoch and Moses, but what about Elijah? He ascends bodily into heaven. Is his "rapture" a type of anyone's rapture?

I propose that Elijah's rapture as recorded in **2 Kings 2** is a type of the conditional Jewish "mid-tribulation" rapture. Please observe that Elijah is a JEW who is alive during a time of **"TROUBLE"** for Israel[20], and the particular **"trouble"** in the land was no rain for a space of 3 ½ years[21] (type of the Great Tribulation)!! Also,

---

[15] **Jude 9 Yet <u>Michael</u> the archangel, when contending with the devil he disputed about the body of Moses…**

[16] **Revelation 12:7 And there was war in heaven: <u>Michael</u> and his angels fought against the dragon; and the dragon fought and his angels,**

[17] **Daniel 12:1 And at that time shall <u>Michael</u> stand up, the great prince which standeth for the children of thy people: and there shall be a time of trouble, such as never was since there was a nation *even* to that same time: and at that time thy people shall be delivered, every one that shall be found written in the book.**

[18] **Jude 9 Yet Michael the archangel, when contending with THE DEVIL he disputed about the body of Moses, durst not bring against him a railing accusation, but said, The Lord rebuke thee.**

[19] The two witnesses are undoubtedly Moses and Elijah, but do not let Elijah's literal reappearance in the future confuse you as to what he TYPIFIES in **2 Kings 2**.

[20] **1 Kings 18:17 And it came to pass, when Ahab saw Elijah, that Ahab said unto him, *Art* thou he that <u>troubleth</u> Israel?**
v.18 And he answered, I have not troubled Israel; but thou, and thy father's house, in that ye have forsaken the commandments of the LORD, and thou hast followed Baalim.

[21] **Luke 4:25 But I tell you of a truth, many widows were in Israel in the days of <u>Elias</u>, when the heaven was shut up <u>three years and six months</u>....**
James 5:17 Elias was a man subject to like passions as we are, and he prayed earnestly that it might not rain: and it <u>rained not</u> on the earth by the space of <u>three years and six months.</u>
Revelation 11:6 These have power to shut heaven, that it <u>rain not</u> in the days of their prophecy....

Elijah is alive during the time of Ahab and Jezebel (type of the Antichrist and Mystery Babylon) and the moment when Elijah was "raptured", there was another Jew (Elisha) right next to him who was <u>LEFT BEHIND</u>.[22] It should be noted that in the historical narrative, Elisha asks for a double portion of Elijah's spirit, and he ends up getting it. As in most types, you cannot match every single detail, and the same is true of this type: the Jews that will be left behind and have to experience 3 ½ years of great tribulation do not catch anyone's mantle and do not get double portions of anyone's spirit. Nevertheless, the salient truth of the "mid-tribulation rapture" is that it is a CONDITIONAL rapture, and in the story of Elijah and Elisha there is indeed a CONDITION given in the text, and it involves LOOKING UPWARD:

2 Kings 2:10 And he said, Thou hast asked a hard thing: *nevertheless,* **IF thou SEE me** *when I am* **taken from thee, it shall be so unto thee; but IF NOT, it shall not be** *so.*

In other words, Elijah was telling Elisha to <u>WATCH</u>. Be sure to notice *THAT.*

---

[22] **2 Kings 2:11 And it came to pass, as they still went on, and talked, that, behold,** *there appeared* **a chariot of fire, and horses of fire, and parted them both asunder; and Elijah went up by a whirlwind into heaven.**
v.12 <u>**And Elisha saw** *it,*</u> **and he cried, My father, my father, the chariot of Israel, and the horsemen thereof. And he saw him no more: and he took hold of his own clothes, and rent them in two pieces.**

18

CHAPTER 4

The "Come Up Hither"-s in the Bible

As will be seen, the phrase **"come up hither"** is directly connected with the truth of the RAPTURE, and it is interesting that the phrase shows up THREE times in the Bible:

1. Revelation 4:1 After this I looked, and, behold, a door *was* opened in heaven: and the first voice which I heard *was* as it were of a trumpet talking with me; which said, <u>Come up hither</u>, and I will shew thee things which must be hereafter.

This **"come up hither"** is spoken to the apostle John and in type will correspond to the rapture of the Church. John is a type of the Church in that he is specifically said to be the disciple that Jesus loved[23], his gospel is the most "Pauline" out of the four, the identity of the man of sin is privately revealed to him, and he hears a voice of a trumpet and is immediately transported into the third heaven.

When John heard **"come up hither"**, he heard it <u>after</u> he saw seven churches whose description remarkably resemble the general condition of the body of Christ over the last 2,000 years. This 'coincidence' is inexplicable apart from the fact that a God who dwells in eternity gave John that information. After John sees the seven churches, he experiences a rapture of sorts and the rest of John's vision deals mostly with the events of the time of sorrows and great tribulation period. The chronology of the churches (**ch. 2-3**), the rapture (**ch.4**), and the time of sorrows / great tribulation (**ch.5-19**) is no coincidence; and just to 'seal the deal' and remove all doubt regarding the PRE-TRIBULATION RAPTURE of the Church, John (by inspiration of the Holy Spirit mind you!) never again mentions the word **"church"** until the very end of the book![24]

---

[23] **John 21:20 Then Peter, turning about, seeth <u>the disciple whom Jesus loved</u> following; which also leaned on his breast at supper, and said, Lord, which is he that betrayeth thee?**
[24] **Revelation 22:16 I Jesus have sent mine angel to testify unto you these things in the <u>churches</u>....**

2. Revelation 11:12 And they heard a great voice from heaven saying unto them, <u>Come up hither</u>. And they ascended up to heaven in a cloud; and their enemies beheld them.

This second point is out of chronological order, but I want to highlight the two commonly accepted raptures before elaborating on the third.

This **"come up hither"** matches the rapture that occurs toward the END of the great tribulation period. In the context of chapter 11, the two witnesses prophesy for 3 ½ years (1,260 days[25]) before they are finally killed by the Antichrist. According to verse 15, this takes place around the time of the 7th Trumpet Judgment[26] which means that their rapture occurs near the end of the Great Tribulation period. In chapter 14, there is evidently another account of dead tribulation saints being raptured[27] which also occurs toward the end of the Great Tribulation right before the battle of Armageddon[28]. It is probable therefore that Moses and Elijah are raptured at the <u>same time</u> as these other dead tribulation saints. These two tribulation raptures of the dead might be separate, but there is no indication that they have to be. To the contrary, there is Biblical precedent to support the idea that both occur at the same time. Consider the account of Jesus Christ's resurrection: This was a notable event in and of itself, but Matthew records that Jesus was not the only one that rose from the dead that third day:

Matthew 27:52 And the graves were opened; and many bodies of the saints which slept arose,
v.53 And came out of the graves after his resurrection, and went into the holy city, and appeared unto many.

With this precedent in mind, I take for granted that the rapture of Moses and Elijah's <u>dead</u> bodies coincides with a rapture of <u>dead</u>

---

[25] Revelation 11:3 And I will give *power* unto <u>my two witnesses</u>, and <u>they shall prophesy a thousand two hundred *and* threescore days</u>, clothed in sackcloth.
[26] Revelation 11:15
[27] Revelation 14:13 And I heard a voice from heaven saying unto me, Write, <u>Blessed *are* the dead</u> which die in the Lord from henceforth: Yea, saith the Spirit, that they may rest from their labours; and their works do follow them....
v.16 And he that sat on the cloud thrust in his sickle on the earth; and <u>the earth was reaped.</u>
[28] Revelation 14:19-20

tribulation saints and this singular event takes place toward the end of the great tribulation period.

3. Proverbs 25:6 Put not forth thyself in the presence of the king, and stand not in the place of great *men:*
v.7 For better *it is* that it be said unto thee, Come up hither; than that thou shouldest be put lower in the presence of the prince whom thine eyes have seen.

It would appear that this passage has absolutely nothing to do with a rapture of any kind. Why would anyone read this and think: "RAPTURE"? Obviously, no one would. It is not until you compare this verse with the other two occurrences of **"come up hither"** that one begins to ponder its implications, and the prophetic application the passage is not seen until one begins to contemplate a third conditional rapture that occurs sometime during the Time of the End.

As will be seen in the pages that follow, the specific condition of this "mid-ish tribulation rapture" is entirely based upon whether a person is READY (i.e. **"WATCHING"**) for the Lord's sudden appearance or NOT. If they DO watch, they will go up to heaven, be with the King, and partake of a marriage feast. If they DO NOT watch, they will be left behind on the earth and have to endure unto the end of the Great Tribulation period. Then, if they manage to survive until the 2nd Advent, they will finally meet their King but will be ashamed at His coming. Being on the earth at the 2nd Advent and not coming down from heaven with Jesus is an indication to everyone that they were disobedient to the Lord's command of watching, and here in **Proverbs 25**, we find the matching elements of that scenario:

v.6 Put not forth thyself in the presence of the king, and stand not in the place of great *men*...

The instruction is to have an attitude of humility, especially when it comes to the KING. During the Time of the End, the individual Jews who have been converted (presumably due to the preaching of the 144,000) will be aware that they have missed the rapture of the Church and have missed all of the blessings associated with it. Throughout history, the Jews have boasted of their unique closeness to God, but now at this time, they must not behave

21

themselves so proudly. They have been in a state of rebellion for over 1,900 years during which time God has directed His attention toward the Gentiles, and has just taken His chosen BRIDE (composed primarily of Gentiles) into Heaven and left Israel in the dust. PRIDE will not get them an audience with the King, but an attitude of HUMILITY might[29], for **"God (the King) resisteth the PROUD, but giveth grace unto the HUMBLE."**[30] If the Jews at this time do not humble themselves, God Himself will humble them:

v.26 For BETTER *it is* **that it be said unto thee, <u>Come up hither</u>; than that thou shouldest be <u>put lower</u> in the presence of the prince whom thine eyes have seen.**

This passage is so closely related to the 3 'feast parables' in **Luke 14**[31] that its instruction is deafening. Once again the context is a KING, an INVITATION, GUESTS, and a FEAST, except the feast spoken of is a WEDDING FEAST:

Luke 14:7 And he put forth a parable to those which were bidden, when he marked how they chose out the chief rooms; saying unto them,

v.8 When thou art bidden of any *man* **to a WEDDING, sit not down in the highest room; lest a more honourable man than thou be bidden of him;**

v.9 And he that bade thee and him come and say to thee, Give this man place; and thou begin with <u>shame</u> to take the lowest room.

v.10 But when thou art bidden, go and sit down in the lowest room; that when he that bade thee cometh, he may say unto thee, Friend, go up higher (i.e. **"Come UP hither"**!): **then shalt thou have worship in the presence of them that sit at MEAT with thee.**

v.11 For whosoever <u>exalteth</u> himself shall be <u>abased</u>; and he that <u>humbleth</u> himself shall be <u>exalted</u>.

---

[29] **Matthew 5:3 Blessed** *are* **the <u>poor in spirit</u>: for theirs is the kingdom of heaven.**
v.4 Blessed *are* **they that <u>mourn</u>: for they shall be comforted.**
v.5 Blessed *are* **the <u>meek</u>: for they shall inherit the earth….**
v.8 Blessed *are* **the <u>pure in heart</u>: for <u>they shall see God</u>.**
[30] **James 4:6**
[31] **Luke 14:7-11, 12-14, and 15-24**

This 'humbling and exalting', and 'being put lower or going up higher' takes on a very LITERAL sense when considered in the light of the Jewish End Time conditional rapture! As a matter of fact, the people that get in on the feast according to **Luke 14:13** are **"the poor, the maimed, the lame** [and] **the blind."** Humility, obedience, and watching are the critical factors that determine which Jews get in on this rapture and partake of the wedding feast.

In **Proverbs 25:7**, notice that a CONDITION is given in that passage too! An End Time Jewish saint can either go up at a RAPTURE (<u>Come up hither</u>) or stay on the ground and be persecuted by the Devil. Hearing **"come up hither"** is certainly the better option but is completely dependent upon each individual End Time saint, and his going up or his staying down is <u>conditional</u> and based upon whether he watches or not.[32] If he DOES NOT watch, he will have to go through the Great Tribulation period and if he survives, he will **"be put lower** (abased or ashamed) **in the presence of the prince"** (Jesus Christ) when he SEES him return at the 2nd Advent.

This shame is connected with the great mourning mentioned in **Zechariah 12:10: And I will pour upon the house of David, and upon the inhabitants of Jerusalem, the spirit of grace and of supplications: and they shall look upon me whom they have pierced, and they shall <u>mourn</u> for him, as one <u>mourneth</u> for *his* only *son,* and shall be in <u>bitterness</u> for him, as one that is in <u>bitterness</u> for *his* firstborn.**
v.11 In that day shall there be a great <u>mourning</u> in Jerusalem, as the <u>mourning</u> of Hadadrimmon in the valley of Megiddon.
v.12 And the land shall <u>mourn</u>, every family apart...
v.14 ...All the families that remain, every family apart, and their wives apart.

The ones mourning here are surviving Jews that are on the ground

---

[32] This concept of WATCHING is emphasized over and over and over in the Kingdom of Heaven passages of the Bible. For the End Time Jewish saint, watching is the KEY to escaping the Great Tribulation period (final 3 ½ years). The Gospels alone are replete with admonitions to WATCH. From Matthew to Luke, there are 19 instances where Jesus talks to the disciples about WATCHING. Furthermore, it just so happens that the admonition to watch is NOT given in John's Gospel! This is because for the Christian, there are no <u>conditions</u> attached to the Church Age rapture! Ready or not, the born again Christian is going UP!

and see Jesus return at the 2nd Advent. Certainly seeing what their fathers did to the Messiah 2,000 years ago, as evidenced by the wounds in his hands, would be cause enough for mourning, but how much more when it occurs to them that they themselves are no better than their fathers? Their fathers had a chance to obey the Messiah, but did not. In fact, the reason they did not obey was because they **"(knew) not the time of (their) visitation"**[33]. In the same way, at the 2nd Advent, those mourning End Time Jews also had a chance to obey their Messiah a few years prior (by watching for Him) but did not know the time of their visitation either! They cannot point an accusing finger at their forefathers and pretend that they would have done better, because the fact that they are on the ground being saved (physically and militarily) is proof positive that they were disobedient, covetous, proud, worldly fools who COULD have obeyed, and watched, and heard Jesus say **"come up hither"**, but did not.

---

[33]**Luke 19:41 And when he was come near, he beheld the city, and wept over it, v.42 Saying, <u>If thou hadst known</u>, even thou, at least in this thy day, the things** *which belong* **unto thy peace! but now they are hid from thine eyes.**
v.43 For the days shall come upon thee, that thine enemies shall cast a trench about thee, and compass thee round, and keep thee in on every side, v.44 And shall lay thee even with the ground, and thy children within thee; and they shall not leave in thee one stone upon another; <u>because thou knewest not the time of thy visitation.</u>

CHAPTER 5

The 3 Major Jewish Feasts

There were three times out of the year that all the men in Israel were supposed to meet together and observe a feast:
Deuteronomy 16:16 <u>Three times</u> in a year shall all thy males appear before the LORD thy God in the place which he shall choose; in the <u>feast of unleavened bread</u>, and in the <u>feast of weeks</u>, and in the <u>feast of tabernacles</u>: and they shall not appear before the LORD empty:
They were specifically told to meet at **"the place which the Lord thy God shall choose"**. This phrase appears only three times in Scripture and is always connected with those three feasts[34]. Furthermore, they did not meet in three different places; each feast was held in ONE PLACE: Jerusalem, just as each rapture will gather God's chosen people to ONE PLACE: Heaven.

These three Jewish feasts match the three raptures perfectly:

1. The Feast of Unleavened Bread (+ Passover)
This feast corresponds to <u>the rapture of the Church.</u>
Passover = 14th day of the first month[35]
Unleavened Bread = 15th - 21st day of the first month[36]

The Passover occurred at a specific time each year, known to everyone. It occurred on the 14th day of the month Abib[37] / Nisan[38]

---

[34] **Deuteronomy 16:6 But at <u>the place which the LORD thy God shall choose</u> to place his name in, there thou shalt sacrifice the passover...
v.10-11 And thou shalt keep the feast of weeks... <u>in the place which the LORD thy God hath chosen</u> to place his name there.
v.13-15 Thou shalt observe the feast of tabernacles...... <u>in the place which the LORD shall choose...</u>**
[35] **Leviticus 23:5 In the fourteenth *day* of the first month at even *is* the LORD'S passover.**
[36] **Leviticus 23:6 And on the fifteenth day of the same month *is* the feast of unleavened bread unto the LORD: seven days ye must eat unleavened bread.
Exodus 12:18 In the first *month,* on the fourteenth day of the month at even, ye shall eat unleavened bread, until the one and twentieth day of the month at even.**
[37] **Exodus 13:4 This day came ye out in the month Abib.**

(which corresponds roughly to early April) during SPRING TIME, just as the rapture of the Church will occur in the spring time[39]. There was no uncertainty as to the timing of the Passover and the date of the Passover may even correspond to the actual date of the rapture. There is a good Biblical possibility that the Lord will receive his Bride physically (Church rapture) on the same day that he received his Bride spiritually (Passover / Feast of Unleavened Bread). The Lord Jesus Christ won his bride the same day his side was pierced; just as Adam received his bride the same day his side was pierced (Adam's side had to be <u>pierced</u> in order to remove his rib!). The Lord will likely take his bride out of "Egypt" physically (Church rapture) on the same day that He took her out of "Egypt" spiritually (Passover / Feast of Unleavened Bread). The date of the Church's rapture, I believe, will be on the same day as the Passover and will commemorate the day that the Lord defeated the Devil (Pharaoh is a type) and **"deliver(ed) them who through fear of death were all their lifetime subject to bondage."**[40] The rapture of the Church will undoubtedly be a MEMORIAL: **Deuteronomy 16:2 Thou shalt therefore sacrifice the passover unto the LORD thy God, of the flock and the herd, in the place which the LORD shall choose to place his name there. v.3 Thou shalt eat no leavened bread with it; seven days shalt thou eat unleavened bread therewith,** *even* **the bread of affliction; <u>for thou camest forth out of the land of Egypt in haste</u>** (no progressive salvation!): **<u>that thou mayest remember the day when thou camest forth out of the land of Egypt all the days of thy life.</u>**

Another peculiar thing in regard to the Passover is the time of day at which it occurs:

---

[38] **Esther 3:7 In the first month, that** *is,* **the month Nisan...**
[39] **Song of Solomon 2:10 My beloved spake, and said unto me, Rise up, my love, my fair one, and come away.**
v.11 For, lo, the winter is past, the rain is over *and* **gone;**
v.12 The flowers appear on the earth; the time of the singing *of birds* **is come, and the voice of the turtle is heard in our land;**
v.13 The fig tree putteth forth her green figs, and the vines *with* **the tender grape give a** *good* **smell. <u>Arise, my love, my fair one, and come away</u>.**
[40] **Hebrews 2:14-15**

Exodus 12:6 And ye shall keep it up until the fourteenth day of the same month: and the whole assembly of the congregation of Israel shall kill it <u>in the evening</u>.
Deuteronomy 16:6 But at the place which the LORD thy God shall choose to place his name in, there thou shalt sacrifice the passover <u>at even, at the going down of the sun</u>, at the season that thou camest forth out of Egypt.

Out of the 3 major feasts, the Passover is the only one in which God emphasizes the TIME OF DAY that it must take place: in the EVENING.

"Oh I am sure it is just a coincidence. A minor, insignificant detail...."

Uh huh. Did you ever notice that when Isaac (type of Jesus Christ) met his wife Rebekah (type of the Church), he met her in the field **"at the eventide"**[41]?

Now take a look at the events of the crucifixion as they relate to the Passover:
Luke 23:44 And it was about the sixth hour (12:00 noon)**, and there was a darkness over all the earth until the ninth hour** (3:00 pm)**....**
v.46 And when Jesus had cried with a loud voice, he said, Father, into thy hands I commend my spirit: and having said thus, he gave up the ghost...
v.50 And, behold, *there was* a man named Joseph, a counsellor; *and he was* a good man, and a just...
v.53 And he took it (the body of Jesus) **down, and wrapped it in linen, and laid it in a sepulchre that was hewn in stone, wherein never man before was laid.**
v.54 And that day was the preparation, <u>and the sabbath drew on.</u>

The Passover was approaching (the 14th day of the month) wherein no one was supposed to do any work, so Joseph had to act

---

[41] **Genesis 24:63 And Isaac went out to meditate in the field <u>at the eventide</u>: and he lifted up his eyes, and saw, and, behold, the camels *were* coming.**
v.64 And Rebekah lifted up her eyes, and when she saw Isaac, she lighted off the camel.

quickly to get Jesus' body off of the cross, wrapped, and buried before that Wednesday High Sabbath began (6:00 pm). Jesus rose from the dead three days later (17th) which would put his resurrection on Saturday evening at roughly 6:00 pm.[42]

Taking all of these things into consideration, it is likely that the Church will be raptured on the date of the Jewish Passover at 6:00 pm which is the beginning of the Jewish <u>evening</u>; or, perhaps the rapture will be 3 days after the Passover at 6:00 pm on the 17th of the month, during the feast of unleavened bread. Since the Lord was **"working salvation in the midst of the earth"**[43] during those three days, one could legitimately argue that the Church did not officially begin until the day of the resurrection (17th), and therefore that day will be the day of the rapture. Whether the rapture of the Church occurs on the 14th or the 17th is really not the issue, the main thing is that it will likely correspond to the timing of the Passover / Feast of Unleavened Bread.

One more significant fact to keep in mind is that 6:00 pm marks **"the going down of the sun"**[44], and when the sun goes down friend, it is NIGHT TIME. Dispensationally and spiritually, the Church Age is likened to the DAY TIME and the Tribulation is likened to the NIGHT TIME.

1 Thessalonians 5:4 But ye, brethren, are <u>not in darkness</u>, that that day should overtake you as a thief.

v.5 Ye are all the <u>children of light</u>, and the <u>children of the day</u>: we are <u>not of the night, nor of darkness</u>.

v.6 Therefore let us not sleep, as *do* others; but let us watch and be sober.

v.7 For they that sleep sleep in <u>the night</u>; and they that be drunken are drunken in <u>the night</u>.

v.8 But let us, <u>who are of the day</u>, be sober, putting on the breastplate of faith and love; and for an helmet, the hope of

---

[42] The subject of the time / date of Jesus' death and resurrection has been thoroughly proven in other works. Suffice it to say, Jesus rose from the dead around 6:00 pm Saturday night but it was not until early Sunday morning before anyone knew about it. By the way, Jesus did not have to wait for the stone to be rolled away before he could get out.; by the time the stone was rolled away, he had been long gone!

[43] **Psalm 74:12 For God *is* my King of old, working salvation in the midst of the earth.**

[44] **Deuteronomy 16:6**

salvation.

The rapture of the Church happens at the end of the "day" (i.e. at the time of the Evening) and what follows is the NIGHT of the End Times which dispensationally extends from 6:00 pm (Evening / Church rapture) to 6:00 am (Morning / 2nd Advent). This "dispensational clock" is very important and will be explained later on in this thesis.

2. The Feast of Tabernacles

I am once again going out of chronological order and skipping ahead to the "post-tribulation rapture" which is what the Feast of Tabernacles is a type of. This feast also occurs on the same exact dates every year:

Feast of Tabernacles = 15th - 21st day of the 7th month.
Solemn Assembly = 22nd day (8th day of the feast)[45]

The Feast of Tabernacles is connected with the 2nd Advent[46] and is also called **"the feast of ingathering"**[47]. At this time, toward **"the end of the year"**, the reapers go through the crops with their sickles and reap the wheat harvest, which is a type of the bodies of the dead tribulation saints being raptured up into heaven. In **Revelation 14** the angels have sickles and are reaping the ripe harvest of the earth[48] <u>before</u> all of the grapes are gathered together to be smashed[49]. The smashing of the grapes is a picture of the Battle of Armageddon, at the very end of the Great Tribulation period, at which time the armies of the nations (who have all sworn

---

[45] **Numbers 29:35 On the eighth day ye shall have a solemn assembly: ye shall do no servile work** *therein:*
[46] **Matthew 17:1-4, Luke 2:16**
[47] **Exodus 23:14-16 Three times thou shalt keep a feast unto me in the year...the feast of unleavened bread** (Passover)**...the feast of harvest** (First-fruits / Pentecost)**....and <u>the feast of ingathering</u>** (Feast of Tabernacles)**,** *which is* **in <u>the end of the year, when thou hast gathered in thy labours out of the field.</u>**
[48] **Revelation 14:15 And another angel came out of the temple, crying with a loud voice to him that sat on the cloud, Thrust in thy sickle, and <u>reap</u>: for the time is come for thee to <u>reap</u>; for the <u>harvest of the earth is ripe.</u>
v.16 And he that sat on the cloud thrust in his sickle on the earth; and the earth was reaped.**
[49] **Revelation 14:17-20, Isaiah 63:1-3**

allegiance to the Antichrist) are destroyed. The fact that the wheat harvest is said to be gathered just prior to the smashing of the grapes indicates that the rapture of the dead[50] End Times saints is just prior to the Battle of Armageddon and also toward the end of the Great Tribulation period.

3. The Feast of Weeks

The **"feast of weeks"**[51] is also called
- **"the feast of harvest"**[52]
- **"the day of the firstfruits"**[53]
- **"the day of Pentecost"**[54]

Try to guess which day of the year this feast occurs on..... You will never guess..... No, really, you will NEVER GUESS because it occurs on a different date each year! The timing of this feast is variable, so they had to WATCH (!) for it.

The way a person figured out when to arrive at Jerusalem for this feast was by paying attention to the crops. The planted crops would grow bigger and bigger as spring time progressed and before long, corn would begin to ripen on the stalks. Once the first ears of corn were grown, the Jews then had to harvest those first ears and take them to the priest. This was not by any means the one and only harvest of the crop, this was simply the FIRSTFRUITS of the crop. They had to WATCH as the crops grew and WAIT until the corn was ripe enough to do an initial reaping. Whichever day of the week the firstfruits were reaped on, they then had to mark the upcoming Sabbath (Saturday) and on Sunday offer the offering of the firstfruits:

---

[50] **Revelation 14:13 And I heard a voice from heaven saying unto me, Write, Blessed** *are* **the __DEAD__ which die in the Lord from henceforth: Yea, saith the Spirit, that they may rest from their labours; and their works do follow them.**
[51] **Deuteronomy 16:10 And thou shalt keep the feast of weeks unto the LORD thy God...**
[52] **Exodus 23:16 And __the feast of harvest__, the firstfruits of thy labours, which thou hast sown in the field....**
[53] **Numbers 28:26 Also in __the day of the firstfruits__, when ye bring a new meat offering unto the LORD, after your weeks** *be out,* **ye shall have an holy convocation....**
[54] **Acts 2:1 And when __the day of Pentecost__ was fully come, they were all with one accord in one place.**

30

**Leviticus 23:9 And the LORD spake unto Moses, saying,
v.10 Speak unto the children of Israel, and say unto them,
When ye be come into the land which I give unto you, <u>and shall
reap the harvest thereof</u>, then ye shall bring <u>a sheaf of the
firstfruits of your harvest unto the priest</u>:
v.11 And he shall wave the sheaf before the LORD, to be
accepted for you: <u>on the morrow after the sabbath</u> the priest
shall wave it.**

On that particular Sunday, the individual was required to bring to
the priest:

1) A sheaf of the firstfruits of his harvest for a wave offering
v.10-11

2) An he lamb without blemish of the first year for a burnt
offering **v.12**

3) Two tenth deals of fine flour mingled with oil for a meat
offering **v.13**

4) The fourth part of an hin of wine for a drink offering **v.13**

Take note that this initial offering is not a FEAST, it is simply a
SACRIFICE. The feast is not for another 50 days:
**Deuteronomy 16:9 Seven weeks shalt thou number unto thee:
<u>begin to number the seven weeks from</u> *such time as* <u>thou</u>
<u>beginnest</u> *to put* <u>the sickle to the corn.</u>
v.10 And thou shalt keep the <u>feast of weeks</u> unto the LORD
thy God with a tribute of a freewill offering of thine hand,
which thou shalt give *unto the LORD thy God,* according as the
LORD thy God hath blessed thee....**

**Leviticus 23:15 And ye shall <u>count unto you from the morrow
after the sabbath</u>, from the day that ye brought the sheaf of the
wave offering; <u>seven sabbaths shall be complete</u>:
v.16 Even unto the morrow after the seventh sabbath shall ye
number <u>fifty days</u>; and ye shall offer <u>a new meat offering</u> unto
the LORD.**

For this **"new meat offering"** they had to bring:
1) Two wave loaves of two tenth deals of fine flour, baken with

leaven for a meat offering   **v.17**[55]

2) Seven lambs without blemish of the first year for a burnt offering   **v.18**

3) One young bullock for a burnt offering   **v.18**

4) Two rams for a burnt offering **v.18**

5) The usual drink offerings   **v.18, Numbers 28:31**

6) For each bullock, an additional three tenth deals of fine flour mingled with oil **Numbers 28:28**

7) For each ram, an additional two tenth deals of fine flour mingled with oil   **Numbers 28:28**

Aren't you glad that you are alive during the New Testament?!

The details of these feasts are somewhat tedious, but the main thing that to remember is that this Feast of Weeks could be held on a different date each year. This is why no specific dates are given. If it was a dry year, and it took a little longer for the crops to grow, that first offering and the subsequent feast of weeks could be pushed out considerably. If it was a very rainy year and conducive for crops, it is possible that the initial sheaf of the firstfruits could be brought to the priest shortly after the Passover and the 50 day countdown would then begin.[56] There was no way of knowing for sure what day the feast of weeks would be on each year until that initial reaping took place, and evidently this was something that the entire nation was watching for; that is to say, since everyone's crops did not ripen on the same exact day, they simply watched for whoever came to the priest FIRST, and the fifty days were counted after that first offering, as opposed to having multiple people bring

---

[55] **Leviticus 23:17 Ye shall bring out of your habitations two wave loaves of two tenth deals: they shall be of fine flour; they shall be baken with leaven;** *THEY ARE THE FIRSTFRUITS UNTO THE LORD.*

[56] It is blatantly incorrect to speculate that the date of the rapture of the Church will be 50 days after the Passover, or that **"those which are alive and remain"** will go up 50 days after the Passover (there are a few variations to this theory). It is incorrect because the feast of Pentecost is NEVER 50 days after the Passover! It is not even 50 days after the Sabbath after the Passover!! As seen above, **PENTACOST HAS NOTHING TO DO WITH THE PASSOVER!!! The date of Pentecost is based upon the date when the first crop of the year is reaped and brought to the priest!** Good grief people, pay attention when you read your Bible!

firstfruit offerings on various days and the feast of weeks being different for everyone. In order for all of the people to be present at the appointed time **"in the place which the Lord thy God shall choose"**[57] and to partake of that FEAST (*get that!*), they were commanded by God to ***WATCH.***

The most outstanding observance of the feast of weeks in Scripture is the one we find in Acts chapter 2. Obviously no one was raptured in Acts chapter 2, but we again find some similar elements. For example, in Acts 2, only JEWS are present, and albeit, the Church Age has technically started, there is no resemblance or mention of the Body of Christ in the entire passage, and the same can be said for the conditional rapture in the future: it is only for Jews and the Church has nothing to do with it.

Also in Acts 2, no one knows for sure when the Lord (the Holy Spirit) will come, but they are WATCHING and waiting for Him. They were commanded **"that they should not depart from Jerusalem, but wait for the promise of the Father"**[58]. They did not know WHEN this would happen and as far as they were concerned, the date of the Holy Spirit's coming was VARIABLE, so they had to WATCH for it, EXACTLY as the End Time Jews will have to WATCH for the sudden appearance of Jesus (not 2nd Advent). The time of the sudden coming of the Holy Spirit in Acts 2 was unknown to the disciples, they had to watch and wait for it, and was conditional upon their obedience to tarry at Jerusalem. In those days, those Jewish disciples who obeyed God's command and watched received POWER from the Holy Spirit[59], and in the future, those Jewish disciples who obey God's command and watch will be RAPTURED into heaven.

"WATCHING" is the key word in relation to this conditional, variable-date rapture that is going to take place sometime during the Beginning of Sorrows. Those who WATCH for the Lord's sudden coming (NOT 2nd Advent) will be raptured up and those who DO NOT WATCH will be left behind. In other words, the

---

[57] **Deuteronomy 16:11**

[58] **Acts 1:4**

[59] They already received the PRESENCE of the Holy Spirit over 1 month prior: **John 20:22, "And when he had said this, he breathed on *them,* and saith unto them, Receive ye the Holy Ghost"**

ones who will go up are the ones who are READY, just like the fruit that is gathered at this feast of weeks is the fruit that is READY; all of the UNREADY (unripe) fruit is <u>left behind</u> and is not gathered until later, during the Fall harvest.

This indicates that there **is someone** who can have a profession of faith and get left behind at **a rapture**; it is just not a Church Age Christian and it is not the Church Age rapture! The ones who will miss a rapture and get left behind[60] are End Time Jews who will not be watching for the Lord's sudden appearance[61] and will not be ready when he comes <u>privately</u> to take them to the wedding feast up in Heaven.

---

[60] If you count the Church rapture, these Jews can technically miss TWO raptures!

[61] **Matthew 24:44 Therefore be ye also READY: for in such an hour as ye think not the Son of man cometh.**

CHAPTER 6

The 7 Raptures

It is worth noting that this early conditional rapture of Jewish End Times saints provides for <u>seven distinct raptures in the Bible.</u> As has been stated before, the word "rapture" does not simply refer to a "resurrection", but rather someone's PHYSICAL BODY being PHYSICALLY taken up into the third heaven to be with God.

The seven raptures in the Bible are as follows and are listed here in chronological order:

1. Enoch

Hebrews 11:5 By faith Enoch was translated <u>that he should not see death</u>; and was <u>not found, because God had translated him:</u> for before his translation he had this testimony, that he pleased God.

2. Moses

Jude 9 Yet Michael the archangel, when contending with the devil he disputed about <u>the BODY of Moses,</u> durst not bring against him a railing accusation, but said, The Lord rebuke thee.
Deuteronomy 34:6 And he buried him (Moses) in a valley in the land of Moab, over against Bethpeor: <u>but no man knoweth of his sepulchre unto this day</u>. (Because his body was taken by Michael)

3. Elijah

2 Kings 2:11 And it came to pass, as they still went on, and talked, that, behold, *there appeared* a chariot of fire, and horses of fire, and parted them both asunder; <u>and Elijah went up by a whirlwind into heaven.</u>

4. Jesus Christ and the dead Old Testament saints[62]

Matthew 27:52 And the graves were opened; and many BODIES of the saints which slept arose,
v.53 And came out of the graves after his resurrection, and went into the holy city, and appeared unto many.

5. The Church

Occurs before the Time of the End.

1 Thessalonians 4:16 For the Lord himself shall descend from heaven with a shout, with the voice of the archangel, and with the trump of God: and the dead in Christ shall rise first:
v.17 Then we which are alive *and* remain shall be caught up together with them in the clouds, to meet the Lord in the air: and so shall we ever be with the Lord.

6. Living Jewish End Time saints who watch and are ready

Occurs sometime during the Beginning of Sorrows.

Matthew 25:10 And while they went to buy, the bridegroom came; and they that were ready went in with him to the marriage: and the door was shut.

7. Moses and Elijah + the dead Jewish End Time saints

Occurs toward the end of the 3 ½ year Great Tribulation period.

Revelation 11:12 And they heard a great voice from heaven saying unto them, Come up hither. And they ascended up to heaven in a cloud; and their enemies beheld them.

Since a long discourse and examination of these seven raptures is beyond the scope of this thesis, this chapter is limited to simply a listing of them.

---

[62] The rapture of the dead Old Testament saints is included with Jesus Christ's resurrection / rapture because both raptures happened around the same time and were probably even simultaneous.

CHAPTER 7

"Watchman, what of the NIGHT?"[63]

In order to get all of this eschatological information to come together, there are still a few details that need to be considered in regard to:
- The role of the 144,000 and when they are sealed
- The length of the Time of the End (3 ½ years, 7 years, etc....)
- The various responses of the Jews in regard to Jesus' command to watch
- The End Time doctrine in the letters to the 7 churches
- The timing of the Man of Sin's appearance in the Holy Place

There is little use in advocating a conditional rapture of living Jewish End Time saints if there is uncertainty as to the LENGTH of the Time of the End. When would this rapture occur? "Pre-tribulation", "mid-tribulation" and "post-tribulation" are meaningless without a frame of reference to base those terms off of, so to find this frame of reference, we will begin with elaborating a little more on the subject of the of the Time of the End being likened to NIGHT TIME.[64]

1 Thessalonians 5:1 But of the times and the seasons, brethren, ye have no need that I write unto you.
v.2 For yourselves know perfectly that <u>the day of the Lord</u> so cometh as a thief in the <u>NIGHT.</u>
Notice that it says **"the day of the Lord"**, NOT "the day of Christ", and NOT "the rapture of the Church". This is an END TIME passage and is directly connected with NIGHT TIME. Prophetically speaking, the Church is raptured out at the time of the Evening watch (6:00 pm) and this event marks the beginning of

---

[63] **Isaiah 21:11**
[64] Yes, the Church is like the moon, and I know about **Romans 13:12**, but that verse is not a dispensational statement; it is a spiritual allegory highlighting the fact that Christians have come out of spiritual DARKNESS into spiritual LIGHT. Besides, if the Church Age is likened to two days (**2 Peter 3:8, John 11:6**) how can the entire Church Age be likened to NIGHT? There would have to be at least TWO days and TWO nights.

the 4 watches of the night of the End Times (a total of 12 'prophetic hours'). The entire length of time from the rapture of the Church to the 2nd Advent is likened to the NIGHT and DARKNESS, and concludes with the physical return of Jesus Christ which is likened to sun coming up in the MORNING.[65]

After a long dissertation on **"the sign of** [the Lord's] **coming, and of the end of the world"**[66], Jesus warns the disciples, **"WATCH ye therefore: for ye know not when the master of the house cometh, at <u>even</u>, or at <u>midnight,</u> or at the <u>cockcrowing</u>, or in the <u>morning</u>: Lest coming suddenly he find you sleeping."**[67]

The ENTIRE CONTEXT here is the End Times; how so many preachers are able to completely misapply this verse to Church Age Christians and teach that this verse PROVES that we cannot know the day or the hour of the rapture is **"too wonderful for me"**[68]! All that can be said for that nonsense is *"good preaching doesn't always make for good doctrine"*.

In this END TIME context, Jesus draws our attention to four watches of the NIGHT:

Evening	6 pm - 9 pm
Midnight	9 pm - 12 am
Cockcrowing	12 am - 3 am
Morning	3 am - 6 am

He then advises the JEWS to watch because THEY do not know **"what hour their Lord doth come".** Well come on now, if He is referring to the 2nd Advent, they *sure do know* when He is

---

[65] Malachi 4:2 But unto you that fear my name shall the Sun of righteousness arise with healing in his wings;

Genesis 19:15 And when the <u>morning</u> arose....

v.23 The <u>sun was risen</u> upon the earth when Lot entered into Zoar.

v.24 Then the LORD rained upon Sodom and upon Gomorrah brimstone and fire from the LORD out of heaven; (this fire from heaven is a type of the 2nd Advent)

Joel 2:1 Blow ye the trumpet in Zion, and sound an alarm in my holy mountain: let all the inhabitants of the land tremble: for the day of the LORD cometh, for *it is* nigh at hand;

v.2 A day of darkness and of gloominess, a day of clouds and of thick darkness, <u>as the morning</u> spread upon the mountains:

[66] Matthew 24:3

[67] Mark 13:35-36

[68] Proverbs 30:18

38

coming! Any Bible Believing Jew living in the End Times could know the time of the 2nd Advent down to the DAY! He would simply have to add 3 ½ years (1,260 days) to the day that the Abomination of Desolation stood in the Holy Place and he would have the date of Christ's 2nd Advent. Any Jew with a working calculator (which may actually prove to be difficult at that time) could determine the exact date of the Lord's return. After all, the Holy Spirit told them no less than FIVE SPECIFIC TIMES the date of the 2nd Advent!

Daniel 12:6 And *one* said to the man clothed in linen, which *was* upon the waters of the river, How long *shall it be to* the end of these wonders?

v.7 And I heard the man clothed in linen…that *it shall be* for a <u>time, times, and an half</u>; and when he shall have accomplished to scatter the power of the holy people, all these *things* shall be finished.

Revelation 11:2 But the court which is without the temple leave out, and measure it not; for it is given unto the Gentiles: and the holy city shall they tread under foot <u>forty *and* two months.</u>

Revelation 12:6 And the woman fled into the wilderness, where she hath a place prepared of God, that they should feed her there <u>a thousand two hundred *and* threescore days.</u>

Revelation 12:14 And to the woman were given two wings of a great eagle, that she might fly into the wilderness, into her place, where she is nourished for <u>a time, and times, and half a time,</u> from the face of the serpent.

Revelation 13:5 And there was given unto him a mouth speaking great things and blasphemies; and power was given unto him to continue <u>forty *and* two months.</u>

The admonition about WATCHING has absolutely NOTHING to do with the Lord's <u>2nd Advent</u>. Even if a Jew in the Time of the End was not watching for the 2nd Advent, his eyes would be instantly turned upward when the universe above his head starts blowing to pieces like a firecracker! So what would be the point in telling anyone to WATCH for the 2nd advent? THE WHOLE WORLD WILL SEE IT!!

Revelation 1:7 Behold, he cometh with clouds; and EVERY EYE shall see him....

The verses that talk about watching for the return of the Lord cannot possibly be referring to the 2nd Advent and they cannot possibly be referring to the rapture of the Church. Therefore, they MUST be referring to something else that commentators and Bible expositors have apparently missed over the last 2,000 years: these verses are referring to a rapture that End Time Jews can be a part of, but only if they are ready at the instant Jesus comes for them.

The exact timing of this rapture is not given and the exact hour cannot be known because its date is slightly variable, just as the date of the Feast of Weeks is slightly variable. This is why the Jews are told over and over in the Kingdom of Heaven gospels (Matthew, Mark and Luke) to WATCH. Thankfully, the Lord gives them a hint as to the approximate timing of this rapture, and by comparing Scripture with Scripture, the specific watch of the night this rapture occurs in is revealed:

In Mark's account, 4 watches are listed:
Mark 13:35 Watch ye therefore: for ye know not when the master of the house cometh, at even (first watch)**, or at midnight** (second watch)**, or at the cockcrowing** (third watch)**, or in the morning** (fourth watch)**....**

In Luke's account, 2 watches are listed:
Luke 12:37 Blessed *are* those servants, whom the lord when he cometh shall find watching.....
v.38 And if he shall come in the second watch (midnight)**, or come in the third watch** (cockcrowing)**, and find *them* so, blessed are those servants.**

In Matthew's account, 1 watch is listed:
Matthew 25:6 And at midnight there was a cry made, Behold, the bridegroom cometh; go ye out to meet him.
40

Remember, the Time of the End, from the rapture of the Church to the 2nd Advent is likened to the Night, so the term **"midnight"** does not necessarily mean 12:00 am on a specific, literal day. We are dealing with the JEWISH concept of night watches rather than a GENTILE designation of a specific hour. The Jewish Midnight watch extends from 9:00 pm to 12:00 am.

On 'God's time clock' the rapture of the Church occurs at 6:00 pm at the start of the EVENING[69] watch. The 2nd Advent occurs at 6:00 am at the end of the Night, at the end of the MORNING watch, at the dawning of the new Day[70]. This means that the entire Time of the End spans all 12 hours of the Night, and the conditional rapture of End Time Jewish saints will occur sometime between 9:00 pm and 12:00 am during the prophetic Midnight watch.

---

[69] **Genesis 24:63   And Isaac went out to meditate in the field at the <u>EVENTIDE</u>: and he lifted up his eyes, and saw, and, behold, the camels *were* coming.**
v.64   And Rebekah lifted up her eyes, and when she saw Isaac, she lighted off the camel.
[70] i.e. the Millennium. **Hebrews 4:8 For if Jesus had given them rest, then would he not afterward have spoken of another <u>day</u>.**

41

CHART 2

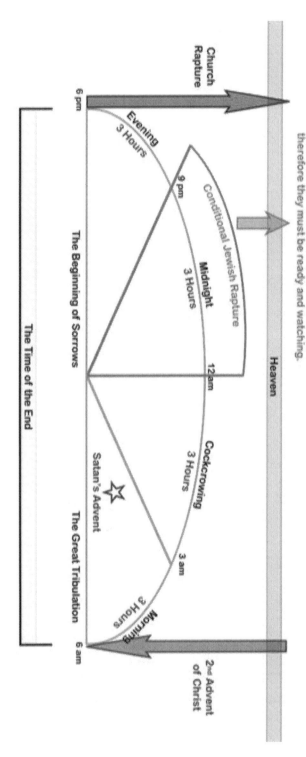

The rapture of the Jewish saints could happen at any time during this Midnight Watch, therefore they must be ready and watching.

Church Rapture

Heaven

Conditional Jewish Rapture

Evening 3 Hours

9 pm

Midnight 3 Hours

12am

Cockcrowing 3 Hours

3 am

Morning 3 Hours

6 am

6 pm

Satan's Advent ☆

The Beginning of Sorrows

The Great Tribulation

The Time of the End

2nd Advent of Christ

CHAPTER 8

The Right Interpretation of Daniel 9:27

There are all kinds of theories as to the length of time that spans from the rapture of the Church to the 2nd Advent of Jesus Christ. Some teach that the End Time is 7 years long; some teach that it is slightly more than 3 ½ years long; some teach that it is 40 years long; some have even gone so far as to say that anyone who believes in a 3 ½ year long Time of the End must also automatically believe in a mid-Tribulation rapture of the Church. Practically ALL of this confusion and debate can be traced back to one thing: **what is the right interpretation of Daniel 9:24-27?** The answer to this question directly or indirectly affects every aspect of interpretation and categorization of End Time events.

v.24 Seventy weeks are determined upon thy people and upon thy holy city, to finish the transgression, and to make an end of sins, and to make reconciliation for iniquity, and to bring in everlasting righteousness, and to seal up the vision and prophecy, and to anoint the most Holy.

This passage is THE SINGULAR FOUNDATION of the popular 7 year tribulation theory and without **Daniel 9:24-27** the 7 year tribulation theory completely disintegrates.

We Bible Believers all agree that the 70 weeks are a reference to prophetic weeks that amount to 490 years, not 70 literal weeks that amount to 490 days. Also, we all agree that the Millennium begins when the 70 prophetic weeks are fulfilled.

v.25 Know therefore and understand, *that* from the going forth of the commandment to restore and to build Jerusalem unto the Messiah the Prince *shall be* seven weeks, and threescore and two weeks: the street shall be built again, and the wall, even in troublous times.

Nehemiah was the one commissioned to rebuild the CITY of Jerusalem and he was the one who rebuilt the WALL during troublous times. Therefore, the 70 week countdown begins around the time of Nehemiah. A number of very scholarly works have been written that attempt to pinpoint the actual year that the 70 prophetic weeks began on, but it is beyond the scope of this thesis to get into those specifics. Suffice it to say, Daniel 'nailed it' and his prophecy of the time between the rebuilding of Jerusalem to Messiah the Prince was accurate down to the exact year.

It should also be noted that the prophecy was not from the rebuilding of the walls of Jerusalem to the BIRTH of Jesus, nor to the TRIUMPHAL ENTRY of Jesus, nor to the CRUCIFIXION of Jesus, but rather to the ANOINTING of Jesus. The word **"Messiah"** and **"Christ"** means "anointed one", and Jesus was not ANOINTED at His birth, nor was He ANOINTED at the triumphal entry into Jerusalem, nor was He ANOINTED at His crucifixion; He was ANOINTED at His baptism[71] when He was about 30 years old[72]. Since Daniel's prophecy was to **"MESSIAH the Prince"** and not simply "the Son of God" or "the Prince, the meaning is clear: Daniel's 70th week BEGAN, not at the BIRTH, TRIUMPHAL ENTRY or CRUCIFIXION of Jesus, but rather at the BAPTISM of Jesus Christ. His ANOINTING indicated that He indeed was the **"MESSIAH"**. Interestingly enough, it was at Jesus' baptism that John identified Jesus as **"the LAMB of God, which taketh away the sin of the world"**[73], a statement which instantly brings to the Jewish mind thoughts of the Passover lamb.

We know from Exodus chapter 12 that the Jews were supposed to sacrifice the Passover lamb on the 14th day of the month in the evening[74], but did you ever notice the peculiar detail about when their lamb was supposed to arrive?

Exodus 12:3   Speak ye unto all the congregation of Israel, saying, <u>In the tenth _day_ of this month they shall take to them</u>

---

[71] **Matthew 3:16 And Jesus, when he was baptized, went up straightway out of the water: and, lo, the heavens were opened unto him, and he saw the Spirit of God descending like a dove, and lighting upon him:**

v.17 And lo a voice from heaven, saying, This is my beloved Son, in whom I am well pleased.

[72] **Luke 3:23 And Jesus himself began to be <u>about thirty years of age</u>...**

[73] **John 1:29**

[74] **Exodus 12:6 And ye shall keep it up until <u>the fourteenth day</u> of the same month: and the whole assembly of the congregation of Israel shall kill it <u>in the evening</u>.**

44

every man a lamb, according to the house of *their* fathers, a lamb for an house:

Why the 10th day? Why does it even matter what day the lamb arrives?! Consider this: if we take the Jewish day/ night timing method[75] into account, the lamb arrives sometime during the <u>day time</u> of the 10th day, and is to be sacrificed on the 14th day <u>in the evening</u>. Take a wild guess how many days that lamb was around for....

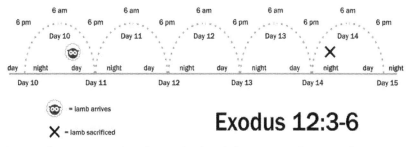

Exodus 12:3-6

As can be seen on the chart, the lamb is present for 3 ½ days! How strange. Why would *that* be? The obvious truth that is staring us straight in the face is that the 3 ½ days of the Passover lamb corresponds to the 3 ½ years of the ministry of **"Christ our passover"**[76]! The first 3 ½ years of Daniel's 70th week was indeed fulfilled during the 3 ½ years of Jesus' ministry.

v.26 And after threescore and two weeks...

Here the verse mentions 62 weeks (434 years) but taking **v.25** into consideration, we know that 7 weeks came first, and then 62 weeks follow. So when it says **"after threescore and two weeks"** we know it to be a total of 69 weeks (7 + 62 = 69) or 483 years, leaving only 1 week (7 years) left to be fulfilled.

...shall Messiah be cut off, but not for himself...

This is obviously a reference to the crucifixion of Jesus Christ for sinners.

...and the people of the prince that shall come shall destroy the city and the sanctuary;...

---

[75] The Jewish method of reckoning days traces back to Genesis. The new day begins in the evening at 6:00 pm and extends 24 hours to the following evening at 6:00 pm, as opposed to the Gentile method of beginning each day at 12:00 midnight.

[76] **1 Corinthians 5:7 ... For even Christ our passover is sacrificed for us...**

This is not necessarily a DIRECT prophetic reference to Titus and the Romans destroying the Temple and Jerusalem in AD 70, although that can certainly be considered as a TYPE or SHADOW of what Daniel is referring to. The DIRECT fulfillment of this prophecy is still future and will be fulfilled by the Antichrist around the start of the Great Tribulation (i.e. the final 3 ½ years of the Time of the End).

The **"prince"** mentioned here is the Antichrist and is not **"Messiah the Prince"** as evidenced by the fact that your King James Bible capitalized one "P" and not the other "p" in the same context[77]!

...and <u>the end</u> thereof *shall be* with a flood, and unto <u>the end</u> of the war desolations are determined.

The frequent use of the phrase **"the end"** indicates that the direct application of this prophecy must be to the End Time and not AD 70.

And now for the clincher:

v.27 And he shall confirm the covenant with many for one week: and in the midst of the week he shall cause the sacrifice and the oblation to cease, and for the overspreading of abominations he shall make *it* desolate, even until the consummation, and that determined shall be poured upon the desolate.

And HE shall confirm the covenant with many for one week....
Who is the **"HE"** referring to?

The answer to THAT question determines that outcome of the rest of your eschatological theology. Does the **"HE"** refer to the **"Messiah"** (Jesus Christ) or **"the prince"** (Antichrist)? There are convincing arguments for both sides, but there can only be <u>one</u> **"HE"**. The applications and actions of each individual are so similar that most Bible Believers cannot even tell them apart. Here is a hint though: one **"HE"** is the right **"HE",** and the other **"HE"** is a <u>counterfeit</u> of the real **"HE"**.

---

[77] This is just one more reason why the King James Bible is superior to the 'original autographs'.

The **"he"** mentioned in **Daniel 9:27** is generally taught to be the Antichrist, and for understandable reasons. When reading the passage, it sounds almost identical to other passages that deal with the Antichrist such as **Daniel 8:11, 11:31**, and **12:11**:

Daniel 9:27 And he shall confirm the covenant with many for one week: and in the midst of the week he shall cause the sacrifice and the oblation to cease, and for the overspreading of abominations he shall make *it* desolate, even until the consummation, and that determined shall be poured upon the desolate.

Daniel 8:11 Yea, he magnified *himself* even to the prince of the host, and by him the daily *sacrifice* was taken away, and the place of his sanctuary was cast down.

Daniel 11:31 And arms shall stand on his part, and they shall pollute the sanctuary of strength, and shall take away the daily *sacrifice*, and they shall place the abomination that maketh desolate.

Daniel 12:11 And from the time *that* the daily *sacrifice* shall be taken away, and the abomination that maketh desolate set up, *there shall be* a thousand two hundred and ninety days.

Practically all commentators link all four verses together and attribute them to the Antichrist without batting an eye. What they failed to notice though is the subtle difference between **Daniel 9:27** and the other three verses.

Have you ever noticed that **"abominations"** is PLURAL in **Daniel 9:27** but SINGULAR in the other three passages?

Have you ever noticed that the sacrifice and oblation is said to **"cease"** in **Daniel 9:27**, but the other three passages say **"taken away"**?

Daniel 8:11, 11:31, and **12:11** are likely talking about the Antichrist[78], their contexts bear witness to that; but when we come to **Daniel 9:27**, we need to be careful and slow down because we

---

[78] **Daniel 11:31** could be exclusively referring to the actions of Antiochus Epiphanes around 162 BC and not the Antichrist.

have another character in the context, **"Messiah the Prince"**, and as Daniel chapter 11 proves, we need to be very wary of the word **"he"**. **"He"** in the book of Daniel can be <u>very</u> tricky. In Daniel chapter 11, **"he"** and **"his"** refer to no less than 6 different characters, and the identity of the **"he"** can switch without warning[79]; so when we come to the word **"he"** in **Daniel 9:27**, we must be careful about <u>assuming</u> who the **"he"** refers to.

I contend that the **"he"** in **Daniel 9:27** is a reference to the **"Messiah"**, Jesus Christ. Pay attention to the sentence structure in the passage: the **"he"** in **Daniel 9:27** is the SUBJECT of the sentence. The **"And"** refers the subject back to someone in the previous verse, and the only two persons in the previous verse are **"Messiah"** and **"the prince"** (Antichrist). The **"he"** (subject) is <u>likely</u> not referring to **"the prince"** because **"the prince"** is the object of a prepositional phrase, and <u>generally</u> in proper English grammar, a SUBJECT does not refer to the object of a prepositional phrase, but rather the previous subject. Prepositional phrases are additional details that can be removed and not affect a sentence grammatically. That is, you could technically read verses 26-27 as follows:

"And after threescore and two weeks shall <u>Messiah</u> be cut off, but not for himself: and the people____shall destroy the city and the sanctuary; and the end thereof *shall be* with a flood, and unto the end of the war desolations are determined.

And <u>HE</u> shall confirm the covenant..."

The sentence structure is still intact and the meaning of the verse is still understood, it is simply missing the additional prepositional phrase, which if omitted, still directs the subject of **v.27** (**"he"**) with the subject of **v.26 "Messiah"**.

The sentence structure of **Daniel 9:26-27** is not a conclusive argument, for it is true that there are exceptions to this general rule and there are indeed multiple instances in the Bible where a subject <u>does</u> refer back to the object of a prepositional phrase. The grammatical aspect of the verse is worthy of consideration, but there are much stronger arguments to prove that the Messiah is the focus of **v. 27.** The undeniable cross references connecting Jesus

---

[79] If you do not believe me, read Daniel chapter 11 sometime!

Christ to **Daniel 9:27** will provide ample proof to the reader that this passage is not talking about the Antichrist, but rather Jesus Christ:

v.27 And he (Jesus Christ) **shall <u>confirm</u> the COVENANT…**
   What **"covenant"** is Daniel talking about? Most expositors say that it is a 7 year peace accord that the Antichrist makes with the nation of Israel but then breaks after 3 ½ years. Perhaps, but notice that the covenant is being CONFIRMED, not MADE. This is not a NEW covenant, but rather a CONFIRMATION of a previously existing covenant. The covenant here in **Daniel 9:27** is NOT a peace accord between the nation of Israel and the Antichrist and Death and Hell[80], but rather a <u>validation</u> of the covenant that God gave to Abraham some 1,500 years prior! This is a reference to the ABRAMIC COVENANT, not the ANTICHRIST'S COVENANT.
   Let us compare Scripture with Scripture, ok?
Galatians 3:17 And this I say, *that* **the <u>covenant</u>** (Abramic)**, that was <u>CONFIRMED</u> before of God <u>in Christ</u>, the law, which was four hundred and thirty years after, cannot disannul** (that is, the OT Law cannot disannul the Abramic Covenant)**, that it should make the promise** (Abramic Covenant) **of none effect.**
   The appearance of the **"Messiah"** on the earth was a CONFIRMATION of the <u>promise</u> / <u>covenant</u> that God made with Abraham a long, long time ago.

Romans 15:8 Now I say that <u>Jesus Christ</u> was a minister of the circumcision for the truth of God, <u>to CONFIRM the promises</u> *<u>made</u>* <u>unto the fathers</u>:
   The **"promises made unto the fathers"** are the promises that

---

[80] **Isaiah 28:15 Because ye have said, We have made a <u>covenant with death</u>, and with hell are we at agreement; when the overflowing scourge shall pass through, it shall not come unto us: for we have made lies our refuge, and under falsehood have we hid ourselves...**
v.18 And your <u>covenant with death</u> shall be disannulled, and your agreement with hell shall not stand; when the overflowing scourge shall pass through, then ye shall be trodden down by it.

God made to Abraham (i.e. the Abramic covenant[81]), and Jesus Christ came for the specific purpose of CONFIRMING that covenant to the Jewish people! Had they accepted Him, the physical promises of that covenant would have been fulfilled and in short time Rome would have been overthrown, Israel would have received their kingdom, and the Jewish race would multiply as the sand of the sea and the stars of heaven for ever and ever.[82]

Psalm 105:8 He hath remembered his <u>covenant</u> for ever, the word *which* he commanded to a thousand generations.
v.9 Which _covenant_ he made with <u>Abraham</u>, and his oath unto Isaac;
v.10 And <u>CONFIRMED</u> the same unto Jacob for a law, *and* to Israel *for* an everlasting <u>covenant</u>:
v.11 Saying, <u>Unto thee will I give the land of Canaan</u>, the lot of your inheritance:

Question: When did God CONFIRM the Abramic covenant to Jacob? The covenant about God multiplying Abram's seed and giving him the land of Canaan for an inheritance was in effect whether Jacob was aware of it or not, but the Bible says that at some point God CONFIRMED it to Jacob. When?

Answer: In the vision of Jacob's ladder:

Genesis 28:12 And he dreamed, and behold a ladder set up on the earth, and the top of it reached to heaven: and behold the angels of God ascending and descending on it.
v.13 And, behold, the LORD stood above it, and said, I *am* the LORD God of Abraham thy father, and the God of Isaac: <u>the land whereon thou liest, to thee will I give it, and to thy seed;</u>
v.14 <u>And thy seed shall be as the dust of the earth,</u> and thou shalt spread abroad to the west, and to the east, and to the

---

[81] **Genesis 15:5 And he brought him forth abroad, and said, Look now toward heaven, and tell the stars, if thou be able to number them: and he said unto him, <u>So shall thy seed be.</u>**
v.6 And he believed in the LORD; and he counted it to him for righteousness.
v.7 And he said unto him, I *am* the LORD that brought thee out of Ur of the Chaldees, <u>to give thee this land to inherit it.</u>

[82] This is an extreme over simplification and omits a vast number of details, but it is not my intent to include here a lengthy dissertation on how history might have unfolded had the Jews accepted their Messiah.

north, and to the south: <u>and in thee and in thy seed shall all the families of the earth be blessed.</u>

God CONFIRMED the covenant that He had made with Abraham to Jacob, and the sign of the CONFIRMATION was the vision of the ladder. Have you ever wondered what a <u>ladder</u> that extends from Heaven to Earth has to do with a <u>covenant</u>? These seem to be two completely separate, disconnected concepts until you get to the New Testament where Jesus Christ reveals that He Himself is that ladder:

John 1:51 And he saith unto him, Verily, verily, I say unto you, <u>Hereafter ye shall see heaven open, and the angels of God ascending and descending upon the Son of man.</u>

There is no mistaking the historical reference to **Genesis 28:12-14,** and when **Psalm 105:8-11**[83] is taken into account, there is no mistaking that Jesus Christ is telling Nathaniel, *"I am that ladder; that sign; that <u>CONFIRMATION</u> of the Abramic Covenant"*. The revelation that Jesus Christ is that ladder and represents the CONFIRMATION of the Abramic Covenant to the Jewish people was a big deal; after all, the Jews had not heard a single word from the Lord in nearly 400 years and they were currently under Roman occupation. Had God forgotten the covenant that He had made with Abraham? Will deliverance ever arise for Israel?! The Jewish people at that time were looking for the fulfillment of God's promises to Abraham. They were in anticipation of the kingdom that God had promised them. Then, at long last, an angel appears to Zacharias and tells him that his wife Elizabeth will have a son whose name is to be John, and shortly after that, an angel visits Mary and tells her that she too will have a son, and his name is to be Jesus. A few months later, when Elizabeth visits Mary, Mary tells Elizabeth, **"My soul doth magnify the Lord, and my spirit hath rejoiced in God my Saviour…He hath holpen his servant Israel, in REMEMBERANCE of his mercy; as he spake to our fathers, to ABRAHAM, and to his seed forever."**[84] As far as Mary was concerned, the virgin birth of Jesus was a sign, a CONFIRMATION of the covenant that God had made with

---

[83] **1 Chronicles 16:15-19** can be added to that as well.
[84] **Luke 1:46-47,54-55**

Abraham. Then comes the birth of John the Baptist, and his father Zacharias was **"filled with the Holy Ghost and prophesied saying, Blessed** *be* **the Lord God of Israel; for he hath visited and redeemed his people, And hath raised up an horn of salvation for us in the house of his servant David; As he spake by the mouth of his holy prophets, which have been since the world began: That we should be saved from our enemies, and from the hand of all that hate us;** <u>**To perform the mercy**</u> <u>***PROMISED*** **to our fathers, and to remember his holy**</u> <u>**COVENANT; The oath which he sware to our father**</u> <u>**ABRAHAM,**</u> **That he would grant unto us, that we being delivered out of the hand of our enemies might serve him without fear, In holiness and righteousness before him, all the days of our life."**[85]

God had <u>not</u> forgotten the covenant that He had made with Abraham, and God's intention was to confirm the covenant and to give the Kingdom to Israel; which is why John the Baptist, Jesus Christ and all the disciples preached <u>repentance</u> because **"the kingdom of heaven is at hand"**[86] (NOT salvation of your soul from Hell by grace through faith!).

As the Scripture bears witness, the Jews rejected their Messiah, but God in his infinite wisdom essentially said *"All right, if you are not going to allow me to confirm the PHYSICAL aspect of that promise (the land), I will confirm the SPIRITUAL aspect of that promise (the seed)[87], and I will re-visit the physical aspect later."*

Back to **Daniel 9**…
v.27 And he (Jesus Christ) **shall confirm the covenant** (Abramic) **with many** (the nation of Israel) **for one week** (7 years)**...**

The prophesied plan was to bring forth the Messiah and within 7

---

[85] **Luke 1:67-75**
[86] John the Baptist: **Matthew 3:2**; Jesus Christ: **Matthew 4:17**; the Disciples: **Matthew 10:7**
[87] **Galatians 3:14 That the blessing of Abraham might come on the Gentiles through Jesus Christ; that we might receive the promise of the Spirit through faith.**
Paul deals with the <u>spiritual</u> aspect of the fulfillment of the promise to Abraham extensively in **Romans 4,9,10,11 and Galatians 3.**

years (the fulfillment of Daniels 70th week) the Jews would have their Kingdom; but that plan ran into a 'snag' thanks to the Pharisees.

....and in <u>the midst of the week</u> (3 ½ years) **HE** (Jesus Christ) **shall cause the sacrifice and the oblation to cease...**

Please notice that the Bible NEVER SAID that there would be 7 years of <u>tribulation</u>. NEVER. People read about "Daniel's 70th week", assume it is talking about the Antichrist, and then hastily jump to the conclusion that there are 7 years of Tribulation. It did not say that. They are reading that into it! By taking a dogmatic stance on a 7 year Tribulation period, the next predictable mistake that many Christians make is this: they say that if anyone claims that there is <u>not</u> 7 years of Tribulation and that there is actually only 3 ½ years of Tribulation, then they therefore must be saying that Jesus Christ's 3 ½ year ministry was the FIRST HALF of the Tribulation Period. Their brain essentially derails itself and cannot think outside of a 7 year tribulation theory. Listen: THERE IS NO SUCH THING AS A "FIRST 3 ½ YEARS OF THE TRIBULATION PERIOD" BECAUSE THERE NEVER WAS A 7 YEAR TRIBULATION PERIOD TO START WITH! There is only 3 ½ years of Daniel's 70th week yet to be fulfilled, and those 3 ½ years are labeled the **"great tribulation"** by Jesus Christ[88].

Because of this erroneous 7 year tribulation theory, the other assumption many Christians make is that if someone says that there are only 3 ½ years of Daniel's 70th week left, then they therefore must be saying that the Church goes through the "first 3 ½ years" of the Tribulation period.

THERE <u>IS</u> NO <u>SUCH</u> <u>THING</u> <u>AS</u> A "FIRST 3 ½ YEARS OF THE TRIBULATION PERIOD"!

There is Daniel's 70th week (7 years) but not all of Daniel's 70th week is tribulation! There was never 7 years of "tribulation" to begin with! There are only 3 ½ years of **"great tribulation"** left to

---

[88] Matthew 24:21 For then shall be <u>great tribulation</u>, such as was not since the beginning of the world to this time, no, nor ever shall be.

be fulfilled and the first 3 ½ years are completely unrelated to ANYTHING involving the tribulation, because the first 3 ½ years of Daniel's 70th week were fulfilled during the 3 ½ year ministry of Jesus Christ.

<u>THERE</u> <u>IS</u> <u>NO</u> <u>SUCH</u> <u>THING</u> <u>AS</u> <u>A</u> "<u>FIRST</u> 3 ½ <u>YEARS</u> <u>OF</u> <u>THE</u> <u>TRIBULATION</u> <u>PERIOD</u>"!

Is that clear? The Bible NEVER SAID there was 7 years of Tribulation UNLESS the passage is interpreted as applying to the Antichrist. Most Bible teachers erroneously <u>assume</u> that the **"he"** in **Daniel 9:27** is the Antichrist which naturally leads them to <u>assume</u> that there are 7 years of Daniel's 70th week left to be fulfilled, and then use circular reasoning to defend their 7 year tribulation period theory. Here is how the argument usually goes:

The tribulation period is 7 years long.
 How do you know?
Because Daniel 9:24-27 says so.
 What if Daniel 9:24-27 is only referring to a 3 ½ year Tribulation period?
It can't be, because the Tribulation is 7 years long.
 How do you know that?
Because Daniel 9:24-27 says so.
 Yah, but what if Jesus fulfilled the first 3 ½ years of Daniel's 70th week, and there are only 3 ½ years left to be fulfilled?
That can't be, because that would mean Jesus went through the first half of the Tribulation during his 3 ½ year ministry.
 But what if Daniel 9:24-27 is <u>not referring to a 7 year Tribulation period but is only referring to a 3 ½ year Tribulation period and the first 3 ½ years describe Jesus' ministry?</u>
It can't be, because the Tribulation is 7 years long.
 How do you know that?!
Because Daniel 9:24-27 says so.
 %&#@#!

v.27 ...and in the midst of the week he shall cause the sacrifice and the oblation to cease...

As stated before, it is possible that these verses can have a <u>dual</u> application to the Antichrist. As a matter of fact, we should expect
54

this to be the case seeing as how the Devil imitates everything the Lord does. The DIRECT application of the verse however, is to the Lord Jesus Christ. After 3 ½ years of His ministry, Jesus causes the Jewish sacrifice and oblation to cease by making it OBSELETE before God the Father. The Jews continued to offer animal sacrifices on the brazen altar for another 37 years after Jesus' crucifixion (up to AD 70), but not a single one of those sacrifices from AD 33 to AD 70 were accepted by God. Jesus' death, burial and resurrection made the sacrifice of the altar completely obsolete, and God the Father punctuated this fact by tearing the Temple veil in half.[89] The blood atonement for sin from that moment forward was found exclusively in the saving faith of Jesus Christ, and from Calvary onward, not a single drop of animal blood could do a single thing for a single person anywhere, anytime!

...and for the overspreading of abominations he shall make *it* desolate...

Whenever this is read, our mind's eye usually looks to the days of the Maccabees when Antiochus Epiphanes sacrificed the pig on the Jewish altar. Then we fast forward and construct a similar scenario happening again in the Tribulation, the new culprit being the Antichrist. There is likely some validity and typology to this, but the DIRECT application is to the Lord Jesus Christ, and do not forget that as far as God is concerned, the term **"abomination"** has a much broader meaning than some irreverent blasphemous act on the brazen altar.[90] Notice also that **"abominations"** is PLURAL in **Daniel 9:27**, and NOT SINGULAR. This little letter "s" is an important detail because it separates **Daniel 9:27** from all of the other seemingly parallel passages in **Daniel 11:31, 12:11, Matthew 24:15** and **Mark 13:14**. **"Abomination"** is not the same as **"Abomination_s_"** and a serious student of the Bible should know better than to simply dismiss this detail.

---

[89] **Mark 15:37 And Jesus cried with a loud voice, and gave up the ghost.**
v.38 And the veil of the temple was rent in twain from the top to the bottom.
[90] Other abominations for example: the froward in heart (**Proverbs 11:20**), lying lips (**Proverbs 12:22**), a false balance (**Proverbs 11:1**), the thoughts of the wicked (**Proverbs 15:26**), and so on.

There were a host of evil deeds being committed by the leaders of the Jewish people that the Lord Jesus found abominable. Seven particular abominations are given in **Proverbs 6:16-19**, and the Pharisees of Jesus' day were guilty of every single one of them:

1. **A proud look**
2. **A lying tongue**
3. **Hands that shed innocent blood**
4. **An heart that deviseth wicked imaginations**
5. **Feet that be swift in running to mischief**
6. **A False witness that speaketh lies**
7. **He that soweth discord among brethren**

Toward the end of Jesus' 3 ½ year ministry, Jesus 'ripped' into the Pharisees over their sins and the book of Matthew devotes an entire chapter of 39 verses that catalogue all of the things they were doing that were ABOMINABLE to the Lord. It is SPECIFICALLY because of the things that the Jewish leaders were doing that the Lord finally draws the line and says: **"Behold, your house is left unto you D-E-S-O-L-A-T-E."**[91]

Game over.

At that moment, God the Father's spirit vacated the Temple. Up until that point, God's presence had been there. Not long before this event, Jesus had rebuked the Jews for making his **"FATHER'S HOUSE"** a den of thieves.[92] It was his Father's house because that was where his Father dwelt! But notice the switch in **Matthew 23** when Jesus said **"Behold, YOUR HOUSE is left unto you desolate."** What he once called His FATHER'S house He now calls THEIR house! Why? Because no one is home anymore; His Father LEFT; it had become DESOLATE. It became desolate at JESUS' WORD; Jesus Christ made the Temple desolate, *just like Daniel said He would.* It happened because of the Jewish leadership's ABOMINATIONS and rejection of their

---

[91] Matthew 23:38

[92] John 2:16 And said unto them that sold doves, Take these things hence; make not my Father's house an house of merchandise.

Matthew 21:12 And Jesus went into the temple of God, and cast out all them that sold and bought in the temple, and overthrew the tables of the moneychangers, and the seats of them that sold doves,

v.13 And said unto them, It is written, My house shall be called the house of prayer; but ye have made it a den of thieves.

Messiah, *just as Daniel said it would be!* The Temple will remain in this desolate condition **"even until the consummation, and that determined shall be poured upon the desolate."**[93] The Temple will NOT re-inhabited by God the Father at any time during the Time of the End. In the near future, whenever the Jews become successful in rebuilding their Temple, the presence of God will NOT fill that place like it did in Moses' day[94], nor will fire from heaven fall upon the altar like it did in Solomon's day[95] UNLESS it is counterfeited by the false prophet[96]. The Temple in Jerusalem will NOT be inhabited by God until it is rebuilt in the Millennium[97].

These things PROVE that 3 ½ years of Daniel's 70th week have already transpired and were fulfilled during the ministry of Jesus Christ, and now only 3 ½ years remain to be fulfilled on God's prophetic clock. That is to say, the first 3 ½ years of Daniel's 70th week were not Tribulation, they were the ministry of Jesus Christ. The last 3 ½ years of Daniel's 70th week will be given to Satan incarnate in the person of the Antichrist, just as the first 3 ½ years were given to God incarnate in the person of Jesus Christ.

Before moving on, an important notation should be made here: just because there are only 3 ½ years left on God's prophetic time clock does not necessarily mean that there are only 3 ½ years of time remaining after the rapture of the Church. In other words, God's prophetic time clock does not <u>have</u> to start simply because the Church gets raptured out. It is perfectly possible for there to be a time gap between the rapture of the Church and the start of the final 3 ½ years.

---

[93] Daniel 9:27

[94] Exodus 40:34 Then a cloud covered the tent of the congregation, and <u>the glory of the LORD filled the tabernacle.</u>

[95] 2 Chronicles 7:1 Now when Solomon had made an end of praying, <u>the fire came down from heaven,</u> and consumed the burnt offering and the sacrifices; <u>and the glory of the LORD filled the house.</u>

[96] Revelation 13:13 And he doeth great wonders, <u>so that he maketh fire come down from heaven on the earth in the sight of men,</u>

[97] Ezekiel 43:4 And <u>the glory of the LORD came into the house</u> by the way of the gate whose prospect *is* toward the east.

CHAPTER 9

Another Gap Theory

[This may be tough for those of you who have not
made it past the FIRST gap theory![98]]

Those that endorse a 7 year tribulation would be quick to say that
*"yes of course, there is a 3 ½ year 'gap' after the Church rapture,
making for a total of 7 years, 'just as Daniel 9:24-27 says'."*….and
we are back to the circular reasoning again. Nevertheless, there
HAS to be some sort of gap between the rapture of the Church and
the <u>start</u> of the last 3 ½ years of Daniel's 70th week. Even die-hard
7 year Tribulation proponents have to concede that if the Church's
rapture occurs during spring-time and the 2nd Advent occurs
during the fall season 7 years later, this TECHNICALLY makes
for a <u>7 ½ year tribulation</u>, not a 7 year tribulation. It has also been
proposed that the time gap might be only a few months amounting
to roughly a 4 year Time of the End (a few months + 3 ½ years).
The one thing that we know FOR SURE is, the chronology
CANNOT exactly and immediately be: Church Rapture, then 3 ½
years, then 2nd Advent. There HAS to be a time gap in-between
the Church Rapture and the start of the final 3 ½ years for a
number of reasons. One reason in particular is that Moses and
Elijah will be given a 3 ½ year ministry[99], and the Antichrist will
also be given a 3 ½ year[100] "ministry"[101], but it is naive to assume
that their ministries begin and end on the same day. They <u>cannot</u>
for the simple reason that the Antichrist outlives Moses and Elijah!
Furthermore, if the Antichrist is killed by the Lord in September
(2nd Advent), and if Moses and Elijah are killed around March

---

[98] **Genesis 1:2**
[99] **Revelation 11:3 And I will give *power* unto my two witnesses, and they shall
prophesy a thousand two hundred *and* threescore days, clothed in sackcloth.**
[100] **Revelation 13:5 And there was given unto him a mouth speaking great things
and blasphemies; and power was given unto him to continue forty *and* two months.**
[101] The word "ministry" is a misnomer really, but you get the point.

(the Feast of Purim[102]) or even December (Christmas), this would mean that the Antichrist outlives Moses and Elijah by 6 to 9 months.

So what? Why does that matter? Answer: If the final 3 ½ years of Daniel's 70th week begins instantaneously at the rapture of the Church, and if Moses and Elijah's 3 ½ year ministry begins BEFORE the Antichrist's 'ministry' begins, and if Moses and Elijah's ministry ends before the Antichrist's ends, this would mean that Moses and Elijah would be alive and preaching for 6 to 9 months DURING the Church Age, BEFORE the Church is raptured!!!

Talk about crossing 'dispensational lines', brother! It is much more plausible and BIBLICAL to allow for a time gap between the rapture of the Church and the start of the final 3 ½ years. After all, a time gap would serve as a 'transitional period' between the Church Age and the Great Tribulation and this "time gap" would contain the events that Jesus described in **Matthew 24:3-14** and called **"the beginning of sorrows"**[103].

Once the length of this time gap is determined, we can then add 3 ½ years (Great Tribulation) and know for certain the length of the entire Time of the End, from the rapture of the Church to the 2nd Advent.

---

[102] **Revelation 11:10** And they that dwell upon the earth shall rejoice over them, and make merry, and shall send gifts one to another; because these two prophets tormented them that dwelt on the earth.
Esther 9:18 But the Jews that *were* at Shushan assembled together on the thirteenth *day* thereof, and on the fourteenth thereof; and on the fifteenth *day* of the same they rested, and made it a day of feasting and gladness.
v.19 ....and a good day, and of sending portions one to another.
[103] **Matthew 24:8** All these *are* the beginning of sorrows.

CHAPTER 10

Satan's Advent

Before I explain the length of the time gap, the reader must first understand when the gap ends and when the final 3 ½ years of Daniel's 70th week begins. Simply put, the final 3 ½ years begins when the Antichrist stands in the Holy Place[104], which I will refer to as "Satan's Advent".

Matthew 24:15   When ye therefore shall see <u>the abomination of desolation,</u> spoken of by Daniel the prophet<u>, stand in the holy place,</u> (whoso readeth, let him understand:)
v.16 THEN let them which be in Judaea flee into the mountains....
v.21 For <u>THEN</u> shall be <u>great tribulation,</u> such as was not since the beginning of the world to this time, no, nor ever shall be.

All of the horrors of the Great Tribulation are initiated by the Antichrist's appearance in the Holy Place (or the setting up of his image in the Holy Place). The importance of this ONE EVENT cannot be over-emphasized. This is <u>THE SINGLUAR PROPHETIC EVENT</u> by which all of the other events in the book of Revelation can be sorted by. This one event is the KEY that unlocks the chorological order of all of the events that occur during the Time of the End.

Notice the peculiar phrase that the Holy Spirit inserted into the verse: **"(whoso readeth, let him understand:)"**. Jesus may not have said this when He was speaking that day to the disciples. I personally believe that when Matthew sat down to write his Gospel, as he was remembering and recording this discourse, the Holy Spirit stopped him at verse 15 and instructed him to insert that emphatic command. This would be the only place in the Bible where the Holy Spirit emphatically stops the <u>READER</u> and tells

---

[104] Technically, I should say when the Abomination of Desolation stands in the Holy Place. The Man of Sin / Antichrist will likely stand inside the Temple and be shot 3 days before the image is set up inside the Holy of Holies, but since the time element between these two things is so close, I will not labor to distinguish the two.

him to PAY CLOSE ATTENTION. There are other places where it says **"he that hath ears to hear, let him hear"**, but this interjection in Matthew 24 is given to the READER; otherwise, if Jesus had said this on Mt. Olivet, He probably would have said "whoso HEARETH, let him understand".

The appearance of the Antichrist in the Holy Place is THE pivotal event of the Time of the End. It is at THIS MOMENT that the Jews are told to flee Jerusalem. This fact alone shows that NONE of the trumpet judgments or vial judgments take place BEFORE this happens. The Lord tells the Jews to run when they see THIS, not when they see monsters coming out of a pit, not when they see 1/3 of all the trees burnt up, and not when the sea turns to blood. Would not such things be a pretty obvious indication that the Jews should get out of Jerusalem? Of course, but Jesus does not point to any of those things, indicating that all of those terrible judgments happen AFTER the Antichrist stands in the Holy Place. The moment that the Antichrist stands in the Holy Place is the moment when God's prophetic time clock resumes, and the final 3 ½ years of Daniel's 70th week begins. All of the awesome, fearful, and horrific trumpet and vial judgments will occur during those last 3 ½ years, giving that time the appropriate title of **"GREAT Tribulation"**.

Also notice that Matthew and Mark advise a hasty retreat, whereas Luke does not. Luke's Gospel gives the astute reader a little bit of a head start; Luke tells his readers in **Luke 21:20, "And when ye shall see Jerusalem compassed with armies, then know that <u>the desolation thereof is nigh</u>.**
v.21 <u>Then let them which are in Judaea flee to the mountains;</u> and let them which are in the midst of it depart out; and let not them that are in the countries enter thereinto."

Matthew and Mark emphasize that the Jews must not even take the time to get an extra pair of clothes, but Luke says nothing about that. The reason for this is, if the Jews leave when they **"see Jerusalem <u>compassed with armies</u>"** (Luke), they WILL have time to grab a few things, but if they wait around long enough to see **"the Abomination of Desolation stand in the Holy Place"** (Matthew and Mark), they WILL NOT have enough time to grab anything, and if they DO take the time to pack a bag, it will be too late and they will not be able to escape the city.

How can this be? How can a matter of minutes make all of the difference? The following is my <u>opinion</u> as to how this scenario is going to play out[105]: After the rapture of the Church, the nations will continue their usual downward spiral of self destruction. Eventually a major world war will break out[106] with Jerusalem being at the epicenter, and once the smoke settles, the United Nations peace keeping forces will have to surround Jerusalem in order to prevent another war from occurring.[107] They are not there to ATTACK the city; they are there to PROTECT the city[108]. This would be the best time for the Jews to leave because there would be no resistance in doing so. However, those who do not leave at this time and ignore Luke's advice will still have one more opportunity to vacate the city. A short while later, perhaps hours, perhaps days, the man of sin will step into the Holy Place. His presence alone will 'desecrate' the Temple, because only the priests are permitted to be inside. Imagine the outrage of the Jewish people! It has been nearly 2,000 years since they have had a temple and then this jerk goes in there! Within a few minutes he comes out, stands at the altar and is shot in the head by an outraged Jew[109]. The city is in an uproar; the Temple has been desecrated, this "high-profile" figure has just been assassinated and now there is a killer on the loose. The UN security forces put the city on LOCKDOWN and no one goes IN or OUT. The assassination of the Man of Sin is a plausible reason as to why Jesus told the Jews in the books of Matthew and Mark to get out of Jerusalem as fast as they can. From the moment that the Man of Sin stands in the Holy Place to the time of his assassination will only be a matter of

---

[105] A whole book could be written about the details of this monumental event, but for brevity's sake, I will only skim over it.

[106] **Revelation 6:4 And there went out another horse** *that was* **red: and** *power* **was given to him that sat thereon to take peace <u>from the earth</u>, and that they should kill one another: and there was given unto him a great sword.**

[107] The first three Seal Judgments (The White Horse, Red Horse, and Black Horse) would have been opened during the "time gap" / beginning of sorrows.

[108] *THIS* time anyway. Jerusalem will be surrounded by the nations of the world TWICE during the End Times, the first time is to 'protect' it, the second time is to destroy it.

[109] Probably a Jew from the tribe of Gad: **Deuteronomy 33:20 + Zechariah 11:17**

minutes. Once he gets hit by that lethal **"bow of steel"**[110], it will be too late, and whoever is still inside of the city is now stuck there. This becomes a major problem for the Jews, because 3 days later, the man that was killed rises from the dead and an awestruck world stares as he walks back into the Temple, this time entering into the Holy of Holies, sits on the mercy seat and says to the world, "I am the Most High God".[111]

This man is now officially Satan manifest in the flesh. There are now exactly 3 ½ years (1,260 days) until the 2nd Advent. The nations of the world, for the first time in history, cease their international wars and unite under this resurrected Messiah[112]. The nations of the world stop warring among each other and declare a united war against the Jewish race. For this brief moment the world cries, **"Peace and Safety!"** but then SUDDEN DESTRUCTION comes upon them, **"as travail upon a woman with child; and they shall not escape"**[113]. Here come 3 more Seal Judgments, 7 Trumpet Judgments and 7 Vial Judgments within a 3 ½ year period of time that will completely devastate the entire earth.

The main thing to keep in mind is this: the final 3 ½ years of Daniel's 70th week begin with the Antichrist standing in the Holy Place, which is what I refer to in this thesis as "Satan's Advent" (**Matthew 24:15**). The rapture of the Church to Satan's Advent is called by Jesus **"the beginning of sorrows"** (**Matthew 24:8**) and the time period from Satan's Advent to the 2nd Advent is called by Jesus the **"Great Tribulation"** (**Matthew 24:21**).

Now that we know when the "time gap" begins (at the rapture of the Church) and when the "time gap" ends (at Satan's Advent), we can now focus on finding out what the length of this gap is, add

---

[110] Job 20:24 He shall flee from the iron weapon, *and* the bow of steel shall strike him through.

[111] 2 Thessalonians 2:4 Who opposeth and exalteth himself above all that is called God, or that is worshipped; so that he as God sitteth in the temple of God, shewing himself that he is God.

[112] Revelation 13:4 And they worshipped the dragon which gave power unto the beast: and they worshipped the beast, saying, Who *is* like unto the beast? who is able to make war with him?....

v.7 And it was given unto him to make war with the saints, and to overcome them: and power was given him over all kindreds, and tongues, and nations.

[113] 1 Thessalonians 5:3

3 ½ years, and ultimately determine the entire length of the Time of the End, from the rapture of the Church to the 2nd Advent.

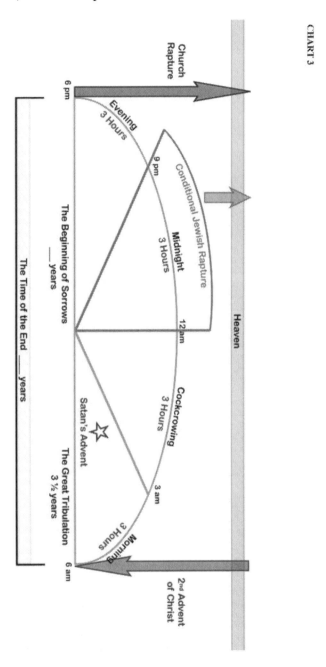

CHART 3

Church Rapture

Heaven

6 pm

Evening
3 Hours

Conditional Jewish Rapture

9 pm

Midnight
3 Hours

12 am

Cockcrowing
3 Hours

3 am

Satan's Advent

The Beginning of Sorrows
___ years

The Great Tribulation
3 ½ years

Morning
3 Hours

6 am

2nd Advent
of Christ

The Time of the End ___ years

CHAPTER 11

The Total Length of the Time of the End

I will state one more time that the "time gap" from the Church rapture to Satan's Advent does not necessarily <u>have</u> to be 3 ½ years, so as to make a 7 year "tribulation". The multiple mentions of 3 ½ years throughout Daniel and Revelation are <u>all</u> talking about the <u>FINAL</u> 3 ½ years of Daniel's 70th week, and <u>none</u> of them are referring to any "first" 3 ½ years:

Revelation 13:5[114]	= final 3 ½ years
Daniel 12:7[115]	= final 3 ½ years
Revelation 11:2[116]	= final 3 ½ years
Revelation 11:3	= <u>Mostly</u> the final 3 ½ years[117]
Daniel 7:25[118]	= final 3 ½ years
Revelation 12:6[119]	= final 3 ½ years
Revelation 12:14[120]	= final 3 ½ years

These last two references are sometimes considered to be "the

---

[114] **Revelation 13:5** And there was given unto him a mouth speaking great things and blasphemies; and power was given unto him to continue <u>forty *and* two months.</u>

[115] **Daniel 12:7** And I heard the man clothed in linen, which *was* upon the waters of the river, when he held up his right hand and his left hand unto heaven, and sware by him that liveth for ever that *it shall be* for <u>a time, times, and an half</u>; and when he shall have accomplished to scatter the power of the holy people, all these *things* shall be finished.

[116] **Revelation 11:2** But the court which is without the temple leave out, and measure it not; for it is given unto the Gentiles: and the holy city shall they tread under foot <u>forty *and* two months.</u>

[117] **Revelation 11:3** And I will give *power* unto my two witnesses, and they shall prophesy <u>a thousand two hundred *and* threescore days</u>, clothed in sackcloth.

As was mentioned earlier, the ministry of Moses and Elijah cannot begin and end on the same day as the Antichrist's "ministry". There is a slight overlap here, but the bulk of Moses and Elijah's ministry occurs during the final 3 ½ years.

[118] **Daniel 7:25** And he shall speak *great* words against the most High, and shall wear out the saints of the most High, and think to change times and laws: and they shall be given into his hand until <u>a time and times and the dividing of time.</u>

[119] **Revelation 12:6** And the woman fled into the wilderness, where she hath a place prepared of God, that they should feed her there <u>a thousand two hundred *and* threescore days.</u>

[120] **Revelation 12:14** And to the woman were given two wings of a great eagle, that she might fly into the wilderness, into her place, where she is nourished for <u>a time, and times, and half a time,</u> from the face of the serpent.

first half of the Tribulation" and the "last half of the Tribulation", but could it be possible that these two verses could be referring to the same final 3 ½ years? Of course they could: both references are about a woman fleeing into the wilderness and being nourished by God. To make them two completely separate events each lasting for 3 ½ years does not make much sense. However, if these are both a reference to the same final 3 ½ years, it would make sense that the first fleeing of the woman corresponds to the Jews that flee at the time that they see the **"abomination of desolation stand in the Holy Place"** and the second flight of the woman are Jews who flee after the Antichrist's slaughter begins. It is interesting to note that Revelation 12 gives the chronology of these events perfectly. The first group of Jews flee in verse 6 which is PRIOR to Satan being cast down to the Earth and the second group of Jews flee in verse 14 which is AFTER Satan is cast down to the Earth. The second group flees specifically from **"the FACE of the serpent"**[121], the reason being that the expulsion of Satan from heaven to the earth occurred between the first and second flights. The first group flees from **"the MAN of sin"** (PRIOR to the Antichrist's assassination), the second group flees from **"the face of the SERPENT"** (AFTER the Antichrist's resurrection). There is an exact 3 ½ year time frame mentioned for the first group (1,260 days[122]), but only a GENERAL time frame is mentioned for the second group (time, times and half a time[123]). This is because the first group flees at the exact moment when the Abomination of Desolation stands in the Holy Place (Satan's Advent), and then a few days later, when the Antichrist rises from the dead and begins slaughtering the Jewish people, the rest of the Jews in Israel flee into the wilderness, each person hiding and then fleeing at various times when it is safe to do so. Thus we have the EXACT time frame of the first group (**Revelation 12:6**), and the GENERAL time frame of the second (**Revelation 12:14**), but regardless, both groups flee around the same time and are in the wilderness for

---

[121] Revelation 12:14 And to the woman were given two wings of a great eagle, that she might fly into the wilderness, into her place, where she is nourished for a time, and times, and half a time, <u>from the face of the serpent.</u>
[122] Revelation 12:6
[123] Revelation 13:14

66

approximately the last 3 ½ years of the Time of the End.

There are only 3 ½ years left to be fulfilled in Daniel's 70th week, and that final 3 ½ years begin with Satan's Advent. In this thesis, **I am going to assert that the total length of the Time of the End is 10 years** (10 ½ years to be exact[124]). There will be a 7 year **"Time of Sorrows"** followed by a 3 ½ year **"Great Tribulation"**.

Allow me to emphasize that this theory is not some lame attempt to reconcile the 3 ½ year theory with the 7 year theory by combining the two together!! That would be an obscene way to reconcile issues of Biblical debate! To the contrary, there are multiple passages in the Bible that indicate a 10 year Time of the End; far more than there are that point to a 7 year, 40 year or ~ 4 year Time of the End. Furthermore, many difficult pieces of the "eschatological puzzle" begin to fit together perfectly once a 10 year Time of the End and conditional rapture of End Time saints is considered and taken into account.

Revelation 2:10 Fear none of those things which thou shalt suffer: behold, the devil shall cast *some* of you into prison, that ye may be tried; AND YE SHALL HAVE TRIBULATION TEN DAYS: be thou faithful unto death, and I will give thee a crown of life.

As of yet, I have not found a Bible commentary that offers an adequate explanation of this verse. Many give the historical application and say that this refers to the 10 imperial persecutions of the Roman Caesars, which is fine, but let's just be honest: where else in your Bible is a "DAY" interpreted as an "imperial persecution"?! From a doctrinal standpoint, would that not fall under the category of **"private interpretation"**[125]?

---

[124] Since the Church Rapture occurs in the SPRING and the 2nd Advent occurs in the FALL which is a separation of 6 months. Many "7 year tribbers" have never stopped to consider that they are actually "7 ½ year tribbers" because of the Spring Rapture and Fall Advent.

[125] **2 Peter 1:20 Knowing this first, that no prophecy of the scripture is of any private interpretation.**

CHART 4

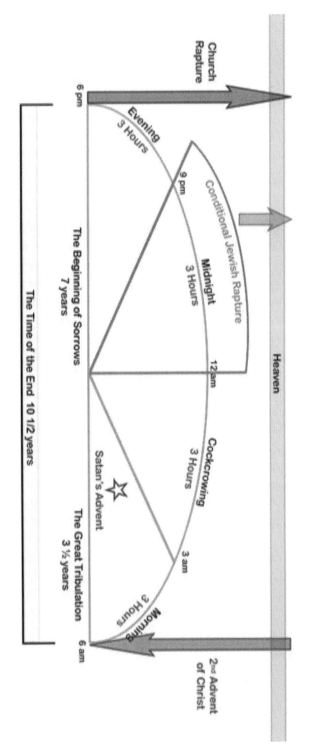

Church Rapture

Heaven

Evening
3 Hours

Conditional Jewish Rapture

9 pm

Midnight
3 Hours

12 am

Cockcrowing
3 Hours

3 am

Satan's Advent

Morning
3 Hours

6 pm

6 am

The Beginning of Sorrows
7 years

The Great Tribulation
3 ½ years

The Time of the End 10 1/2 years

2nd Advent of Christ

68

Another theory regarding this verse is that during the Time of the End, any of God's people who are imprisoned will have a 10 day jail sentence before their execution. This is certainly possible and there even an <u>historical</u> precedent for this: after World War 2, the Russian government persecuted their own people and often condemned their citizens with jail sentences called "tenners" in which people were held in prison for 10 days before being executed or sent to the gulags. However, to say that this is the correct interpretation of **Revelation 2:10** is a pretty flimsy position and is really nothing more than a guess, because once again, there is no Biblical precedent for a 10 day jail sentence that precedes an execution.

There *IS* though, ample Biblical evidence to show that a **"day"** in the Bible can refer to a **"year"**.[126] Given the fact that the verse says **"ye shall have tribulation ten days"**, is it really *that* absurd to wonder if the Time of the End could be 10 years long? Now that we have interpreted **Daniel 9:27** properly, the 7 year 'tribbers' really do not have a Biblical leg left to stand on, and they are certainly not going to find a verse as clear as **Revelation 2:10** that SPECIFICALLY says that God's people are going to have tribulation for TEN days (i.e. years)!

But let us continue.

The 7 letters to the 7 churches contain <u>doctrine</u> that is applicable to people that will be alive during the End Times and there are many things mentioned in those letters that cannot <u>doctrinally</u> apply to anyone in the Church Age. For example:
 - The term **"overcometh"** occurs 7 times[127]
 - There are people who are in proximity to <u>Satan's</u> seat[128]
 - One church is threatened with having its candle taken away[129]
 - One church is threatened with being spued out of the Lord's

---

[126] **Numbers 14:34** After <u>the number of the days</u> in which ye searched the land, *even* <u>forty days, each day for a year,</u> shall ye bear your iniquities, *even* <u>forty years</u>, and ye shall know my breach of promise.
Ezekiel 4:6 And when thou hast accomplished them, lie again on thy right side, and thou shalt bear the iniquity of the house of Judah <u>forty days: I have appointed thee each day for a year.</u>
[127] **Revelation 2:7,11,17,26; 3:5,12,21**
[128] **Revelation 2:13** Not the Pope's seat - SATAN'S seat.
[129] **Revelation 2:5** Ephesus

mouth[130]

Of course, there is spiritual application that can be gleaned from these passages but from a DOCTRINAL standpoint, there are more contradictions to Paul's epistles in these 7 letters than 'you can shake a stick at'.

It is far more likely that these 7 churches represent 7 types or groups of people that will be alive during the Time of the End. All of the letters contain essentially the same doctrinal instruction, but there are different rewards and consequences for the 7 different churches. The Holy Spirit's mention of the 10 days of tribulation to the Smyrna church is <u>deliberate</u> and very instructive, and will be elaborated on shortly.

A 10 year Time of the End theory allows for a pre-Tribulation rapture of the Church, adequate time for all of the events of the book of Revelation to unfold, and a transitional period between the Church Age and the Great Tribulation.

Most Bible Believers are familiar with Biblical numerology and the number 10 is indisputably connected with the Gentiles. A 10 year long Time of the End is appropriate seeing as how the removal of the Church marks the beginning of the end of **"The Times of the Gentiles"**[131], and this final period of Gentile dominion is symbolized by TEN TOES on the image from Nebuchadnezzar's dream[132]. These ten toes are certainly connected with the TEN KINGS that will be in vogue at the Time of the End, but is it really that difficult to recognize the possibility of a dual application here? Could the TEN TOES represent TEN KINGS and *also* indicate TEN YEARS?

Consider some other unusual appearances of the number 10, and see if you cannot recognize some TYPES in the passages:

---

[130] **Revelation 3:16** Laodicea

[131] **Luke 21:23 But woe unto them that are with child, and to them that give suck, in those days! for there shall be great distress in the land, and wrath upon this people. v.24 And they shall fall by the edge of the sword, and shall be led away captive into all nations: and Jerusalem shall be trodden down of the Gentiles, <u>until the times of the Gentiles be fulfilled.</u>**

[132] Daniel 2:42

When **Rebekah** (type: the Church / Bride of Christ) finally meets her bridegroom (type: Jesus Christ), she meets him **"in the field"** (type: the world) **"at the EVENTIDE"**[133](type: prophetic time of the rapture of the Church), and the Scripture even gives the seemingly insignificant detail that **"Rebekah lifted up her eyes, and when she SAW Isaac, she LIGHTED OFF the camel."** We are told in **1 John 3:2** that when we SEE Jesus, we shall be like Him; that is, we shall be CHANGED[134] and CAUGHT UP[135] (lighted off our 'camel', you might say) to meet the Lord in the air! Also, as you may recall, when Abraham's servant was ready to take Rebekah home to be with Isaac, her family insisted that she stay for TEN days (!):

Genesis 24:55 And her brother and her mother said, Let the damsel abide with us *a few* days, <u>at the least ten</u>; after that she shall go.

Rebekah evidently recognizes that her family has been watching a little too much Steven Anderson on YouTube. She does not believe in this post-Tribulation rapture mumbo-jumbo and knows that the Church is not present for <u>any part</u> of the End Times. In a proper display of rightly dividing the word, she tells her family that she is not going to stick around for 10 days, or 7 days, or even 3 ½ days for that matter, but is rather going to leave beforehand and meet her husband at eventide before the NIGHT (type: Time of the End) sets in!

Daniel is another great type of a Jew who is alive during the Time of the End. He is a Jewish captive in Babylon under king Nebuchadnezzar (type: the Antichrist). Daniel determines that he is not going to eat the king's **"dainties"**, for after all, they are

---

[133] Genesis 24:63 And Isaac went out to meditate in the field at the eventide: and he lifted up his eyes, and saw, and, behold, the camels *were* coming.
v.64 And Rebekah lifted up her eyes, and when she saw Isaac, she lighted off the camel.
[134] 1 Corinthians 15:51 Behold, I shew you a mystery; We shall not all sleep, but we shall all be <u>changed,</u>
[135] 1 Thessalonians 4:17 Then we which are alive *and* remain shall be <u>caught up</u> together with them in the clouds, <u>to meet the Lord</u> in the air: and so shall we ever be with the Lord.

71

"deceitful meat" [136] and he knows better than to mess with someone who has **"an evil EYE"** [137] (i.e. the Antichrist) [138]. So he asks to be proven for TEN days.

Not 7 days; 10 days.

Not 3 ½ days; 10 Days.

Why 10 days, I wonder?

Job is another great type of a Jew who is on the ground during the Time of the End, and his book also has some notable 10's in it:

- He has 10 kids
- Job is reproached 10 times by his **"friends"** [139]
- Job is on the ground for ___ days.

Now, I know what the typical 7 year 'tribber' is thinking: *"Ah ha! Job was on the ground for SEVEN days, which is a type of a SEVEN year tribulation!"* Perhaps, perhaps; but did you ever count how many days are specifically mentioned in chapters 1 and 2? Do you want to take a guess?

Job 1:6 Now there was a DAY when the sons of God came...

v.13 And there was a DAY when his sons and his daughters *were* eating and drinking...

2:1 Again there was a DAY when the sons of God came to present themselves....

v.13 So they sat down with him upon the ground SEVEN DAYS .....

I think that $1 + 1 + 1 + 7 = 10$ (!)

Why so many 10's? We Bible Believers know that this is not a superfluous detail; not when we are talking about GOD'S BOOK!

The plagues of the Exodus are a wonderful type of the things that will happen during Time of the End, and it just so happens that

---

[136] **Proverbs 23:3 Be not desirous of his dainties: for they *are* deceitful meat.**

[137] **Proverbs 23:6 Eat thou not the bread of *him that hath* an evil eye, neither desire thou his dainty meats:**

[138] **Zechariah 11:7 Woe to the idol shepherd that leaveth the flock! the sword *shall be* upon his arm, and upon his right eye: his arm shall be clean dried up, and his right eye shall be utterly darkened.**

[139] **Job 19:3 These TEN times have ye reproached me: ye are not ashamed *that* ye make yourselves strange to me.**

72

God brings about 10 plagues on Egypt. Why not 7 plagues? Would not 7 plagues be the 'perfect'[140] number of plagues to bring upon them?

"Oh yes, well, he used 10 plagues because Egypt is a Gentile nation, and 10 is the number of the Gentiles". Verily; so would I be out of line by advocating a 10 year Time of the End given that the **"times of the Gentiles"** are fulfilled (FULL - FILL - ed) at the 2nd Advent at the end of TEN YEARS?

Luke 21:24 And they shall fall by the edge of the sword, and shall be led away captive into all nations: and Jerusalem shall be trodden down of the Gentiles, until THE TIMES OF THE GENTILES be fulfilled. [141]

Over in **1 Samuel 25**, David and a bunch of exiled Jews are out in the wilderness (type: Jews during the Time of the End) and are given a hard time by a guy named **Nabal** (type: the Antichrist). This guy made it difficult for these Jews to get any FOOD.[142] 10 DAYS transpire in the story until at last Nabal is over-indulging himself at a feast when he is smitten by the Lord IN THE MORNING!! (type: 2nd Advent)[143]

Nehemiah rebuilds the walls of Jerusalem **"in troublous times"** (type: Time of the End)[144], and while he is installing 10 GATES, he is threatened 10 TIMES.[145]

---

[140] I say this tongue in cheek. The number 7 is certainly the number of perfection, but God obviously did not want to use 7 plagues; he used 10 plagues 'for some odd reason'.
[141] The **"Times of the Gentiles"** is not fulfilled in AD 70, AD 1948, or at the rapture of the Church, my friend.
[142] Does any of this sound familiar?
[143] **1 Samuel 25:36-38.** Note: if **v.38** is read by itself, it sounds like Nabal was in a coma for 10 days or something and then died, but when **v.37** is carefully considered, it is evident that he was struck dead on the spot, because if your HEART DIES within you, you are DEAD.
[144] **Daniel 9:25 Know therefore and understand,** *that* **from the going forth of the commandment to restore and to build Jerusalem unto the Messiah the Prince** *shall be* **seven weeks, and threescore and two weeks: the street shall be built again, and the wall, even in** <u>troublous times.</u>
[145] **Nehemiah 4:12 And it came to pass, that when the Jews which dwelt by them came, they said unto us ten times, From all places whence ye shall return unto us** *they will be upon you.*

All of this might seem anecdotal to you, but God records these details for a reason, and if you are not convinced yet, let me draw your attention to our next exhibit: **Joseph**.

Joseph is arguably the greatest type of Jesus Christ in the entire Old Testament. There are a plethora of details about his life that match BOTH advents of Jesus Christ, and it is important to notice that the Holy Spirit was very careful to record Joseph's age at the various milestones of his life. When Joseph was sold into bondage, he was <u>17 years old</u>.[146] He was <u>30 years old</u> when he interpreted Pharaoh's dream and was made Pharaoh's vice president.[147] In that dream, the Lord revealed to Joseph that there would be 7 years of plenty followed by 7 years of famine in Egypt.

"Ah HA! A 7 year tribulation period!!"

Hang on, hang on; there would be 7 years of plenty and 7 years of famine in the land, and God said He would **"<u>shortly</u> bring it to pass"**[148]. That is, <u>the 14 years did not start on that day</u>. There is an allowance for a small time-interim there, but we are not expressly told how long that time was. The only way that we could possibly determine that length of time would be by searching the Scriptures and comparing this account with another similar Bible story: Daniel and the interpretation of Nebuchadnezzar's dream.[149] When Daniel revealed to Nebuchadnezzar that God was planning on teaching the Babylonian king a lesson about 'who *really* is in charge', the execution of that vision was not immediate; that is, it would 'shortly come to pass'. <u>God waited for 12 months before he brought the vision to pass</u>:

Daniel 4:29 <u>At the end of twelve months</u> he walked in the palace of the kingdom of Babylon.

v.30 The king spake, and said, Is not this great Babylon, that I have built for the house of the kingdom by the might of my power, and for the honour of my majesty?

---

[146] Genesis 37:2 These *are* the generations of Jacob. Joseph, *being* <u>seventeen years old</u>, was feeding the flock with his brethren....

[147] Genesis 41:46 And Joseph *was* <u>thirty years old</u> when he stood before Pharaoh king of Egypt....

[148] Genesis 41:32 And for that the dream was doubled unto Pharaoh twice; *it is* because the thing *is* established by God, and <u>God will shortly bring it to pass</u>.

[149] Daniel 4

v.31 While the word *was* in the king's mouth, there fell a voice from heaven, *saying,* O king Nebuchadnezzar, to thee it is spoken; The kingdom is departed from thee.

Just for fun, let us go ahead and see what happens if we use this same Biblical time gap of 12 months and apply it to the story of Joseph:

      1 Year (12 months) **Genesis 41:32** and **Daniel 4:29**
      7 Years of plenty   **Genesis 41:47**
    + 2 Years of famine   **Genesis 45:6**
      10 YEARS …… How about that?

This means that when Joseph made himself known the 2nd time to his brethren (type: 2nd Advent), the Bible records 10 SPECIFIC YEARS from the time of Joseph's interpretation to the time of his revelation to his brethren.

Now, I know what some readers are thinking right now:
"Isn't it convenient that this Matt Crane guy made the phrase 'shortly bring it to pass' equal one year? What a crock!"

Fair enough, but before this concept is completely rejected out of hand, let me draw your attention to the fact that if this *is* correct, it would make Joseph 40 years old when he was revealed the second time to his brethren (type: 2nd Advent)!!

Genesis 41:46 And Joseph *was* thirty years old when he stood before Pharaoh king of Egypt.

      Age 30
            1 year   (12 months)
            7 years plenty
          + 2 years famine
      Age 40

Doesn't that just sound like the Lord's timing to you? Isn't it just sound like the Lord to throw a 40 in there? By the way, if that **"shortly"** is anything less than 1 year, then Joseph would have been **39 years old** when he was revealed to his brethren, which is a **3 x 13** (!) and you KNOW that the Lord is not going to make the greatest Biblical type of his Son be connected in any way with a **13**!

One last thought: Why is it that in the book of Revelation so many judgments are connected with **the fraction ONE-THIRD?** Trumpet judgments #1,2,3,4, and 6 all contain disasters that affect 1/3 of things. These trumpet judgments do not begin until AFTER the man of sin stands in the Holy Place (i.e. Satan's Advent), because if the 1st trumpet judgment happened BEFORE the Satan's Advent, should not Jesus have said *"When you see hail, fire and blood fall from the sky and burn up 1/3 of the trees and all of the green grass, run to the wilderness"*?! Why point to an obscure moment when some guy trespasses onto the Temple property and not point to the 1st trumpet judgment? The obvious answer is, the 1st trumpet judgment does not occur until AFTER the Antichrist stands in the Holy Place.

So if there is a 10 year Time of the End and the final 3 ½ years are **"the Great Tribulation"**, then that means **"the Beginning of Sorrows"** lasts for 7 years. In other words, after the Church is raptured, 7 years transpire, and *then* the Antichrist makes his appearance in the Temple at Jerusalem, and *then* 'all Hell breaks loose' for 3 ½ years via 7 trumpet judgments, 7 vial judgments and seal judgments #5,6, and 7.

This also explains the **"sudden destruction"** mentioned in **1 Thessalonians 5:3: For when they shall say, Peace and safety; then <u>sudden destruction</u> cometh upon them, as travail upon a woman with child; and they shall not escape.** They say **"Peace and safety"** at the moment when the world recognizes their FALSE MESSIAH and are deceived into believing that he is going to bring in a FALSE MILLENNIUM. **"Peace and safety"** is what the nations of the world will say AFTER they see the Antichrist rise from the dead.

Revelation 13:4 ....and they worshipped the beast, saying, Who *is* like unto the beast? <u>who is able to make war with him?</u> The opposite of war is PEACE, i.e. **"Peace and safety"**. The nations will STOP their warring against each other at *that* time, however the world's **"Peace and safety"** will be for everyone EXCEPT the Jews! The nations will stop warring with each other and will declare global war against the Jewish race, but their supposed **"Peace and safety"** is short lived because what quickly follows is unimaginable SUDDEN disaster, compliments of God

76

Almighty.

The sum of all these things is this: Since the trumpet judgments begin at the START of the final 3 ½ years and span the entire 3 ½ years of the Great Tribulation, the Lord connects those judgments with the fraction ONE-THIRD. Why? The answer is simple: **3 ½ years is ONE-THIRD of 10 ½ years.** These trumpet judgments are the Lord's way of showing the world that the final 3 ½ years of Daniel's 70th week (i.e. the Great Tribulation) have begun and this Hellish time period is ONE-THIRD of the entire length of the Time of the End.

CHAPTER 12

The Big Picture

When putting together a puzzle, it is important that every single piece be placed not only in the correct spot, but also in the correct position. Every piece has its proper place, and if any one piece is out of position, it will affect the other pieces, and the picture will never be properly seen. God's puzzle of Bible prophecy began as far back as **Genesis 3:15**[150] and God's people have been working on that puzzle ever since. As the canon of Scripture was revealed, more and more pieces were brought out until John penned the last words of the book of Revelation. At that moment, the Body of Christ had all of the pieces, it was then just a matter of putting them all together. The prophetic puzzle was understandably difficult for the early Church fathers, and they made many errors which were later corrected. The puzzle has been worked on by born again Christians for nearly 2,000 years, and now at the end of the Church Age, Christians have the advantage of a nearly complete view of the entire picture. However, there are still a number of pieces missing from the picture and in spite of multiple efforts by multiple Bible teachers, the pieces that we have left do not seem to fit anywhere. Some people have taken it upon themselves to FORCE the remaining pieces into place, and have come up with a 'picture' that shows the Church going through the Tribulation and born again Christians taking the mark of the Beast. The problems with that picture are blatant and obvious to everyone except the people who want to say that they themselves have solved the puzzle! **No theory is above scrutiny.** It does not matter WHO came up with it, or how good they are at putting the puzzle together, each piece must be examined by the student of Scripture. We are told to **"Prove ALL things"** and to **"hold fast that which is good."**[151] We are not told to hold fast that which has been taught BY GOOD PEOPLE, we are told to hold fast that which IS GOOD. That is, even good Bible teachers can make mistakes with

---

[150] **Genesis 3:15** is the first prophecy in the Bible.
[151] **1 Thessalonians 5:21**

78

the puzzle. If we are to only hold fast that which is good, what do you suppose we should do when we find that which is NOT GOOD? Answer: Not hold fast to it; or in other words, get rid of it. There are some pieces in this puzzle that even well meaning Bible Believers have gotten wrong, and the puzzle is now at a point where the picture cannot be assembled any further until we pull out some of the wrong pieces. Respect of persons has always been a hindrance to advancement in Bible knowledge. As soon as someone suggests that a piece does not look right, a cacophony of voices shout *"How dare you say that?! That piece was put there by the great   (Bible teacher name)! Do you think you are smarter than he is?!"* The dissenting voice is then usually silenced and everyone goes back to trying to figure out why the remaining puzzle pieces do not fit.

This ridiculous mentality is prevalent even among Bible Believers, and the only way to overcome this is to shove your way up to the puzzle and begin to rearrange the pieces in spite of the criticism, while reassuring everyone that **disagreement does not equal disrespect.** Most people will think that you are ruining the puzzle by taking some pieces out and rearranging others, but when you can finally show that the picture is now clearer and demonstrate that previously difficult pieces can now start to fit, then and only then will any new theory be accepted with the Bible Believing brethren.

The purpose of this thesis is to deliberately rearrange some of the pieces that have been preventing progress on the prophecy puzzle. The 7 year tribulation theory with its teaching of 3 ½ years of peace followed by 3 ½ years of chaos has served to hinder much understanding of the prophetic Scriptures. When the details of this theory are closely examined, one discovers so many gaping holes that it is incredible that the theory has lasted for so long. In recent years, it has been thoroughly demonstrated that only 3 ½ years of Daniel's 70th week remain to be fulfilled[152]. For over a century the two 3 ½ year puzzle pieces have been forced to fit together and not until recently have those two pieces been separated: the first 3 ½

---

[152] See the book entitled "Daniel's 70th Week" by Pastor Brian Donovan and the thesis entitled "The Blessed Hope" by David Rowley.

year piece has been placed back over in the 1st Advent where it fits perfectly and the second 3 ½ year puzzle piece has been properly left in the Great Tribulation. Progress is once again starting to be made to the puzzle, but now some other pieces are being crammed into places where they do not belong. Some Marriage Supper of the Lamb pieces are being placed in the Millennium area of the puzzle, and a chunk of the puzzle called "the Church rapture" has been moved right up against the 3 ½ year Great Tribulation puzzle piece. I contend that although some of the pieces are finally right, some of these subsequent pieces are wrong and need to be re-evaluated.

In the previous chapter, there were over seven examples given that indicated that the Time of the End was 10 years long. The final 3 ½ years of the Great Tribulation are contained within those 10 years, which obviously means that there is a 7 year time gap (the **"Beginning of Sorrows"**) between the rapture of the Church and the start of the Great Tribulation.

Now that some groundwork has been laid for the possibilities of a 10 year Time of the End and a conditional rapture of Jewish End Time saints, I will briefly give an overview of the entire prophecy puzzle and we will see if the old pieces now fit better than they did before, and if any of the previously difficult pieces can now be added to the picture.

The Body of Christ is going to be raptured out of this world in the very near future. After that, a TRANSITION PERIOD will commence and will last for 7 years. This is a time period that is transitioning from salvation as we know it in the Church age to a FAITH + WORKS set-up during the Great Tribulation (the final 3 ½ years). During this interim, the 144,000 Jewish servants are sealed and sent forth to preach. Notice that they are SEALED[153] (which has a Church Age tone to it) yet they are all JEWS (which

---

[153] Revelation 7:4 And I heard the number of them which were <u>sealed</u>: *and there were* <u>sealed</u> an hundred *and* forty *and* four thousand of all the tribes of the children of Israel.

has an End Time tone to it). These 144,000 are typified in the Bible by JEREMIAH and PAUL which accounts for the Old Testament AND New Testament aspects of their salvation. Notice that both of these men were unmarried, male, Jewish virgins who were specifically selected by God to carry a special message. Paul was spiritually sealed and eternally secure. Both Paul and Jeremiah were rejected by the Jewish people and both of them were commissioned to take their message to the Gentile nations[154]. Jeremiah's depressing ministry had practically zero Jewish people even listen, much less repent, and Paul did not have much success among the Jews either; but when the word of God was taken to the Gentiles, Paul saw great multitudes of them repent and become converted. Paul ultimately was decapitated by a Roman Caesar, whereas Jeremiah witnessed the destruction of Jerusalem and his death is not recorded. All of these details have striking similarities to the 144,000, who are also unmarried, male, Jewish virgins[155] and are sealed unto the day of their redemption[156]. They begin by preaching God's word to the Jewish people, but their message is rejected[157], they themselves are persecuted, and some are even killed[158]. After preaching in Jerusalem and Judea, they then go to the uttermost parts of the earth[159] and preach to the Gentiles who receive the word of their testimony. In fact, the last true revival on earth will be the multitudes of Gentiles who convert under the preaching of the 144,000:

Revelation 7:9 After this (i.e. after the sealing of the 144,000 in verses 1-8) **I beheld, and, lo, <u>a great multitude</u>, which <u>no man could number</u>** (that is a LOT!), **<u>of all nations, and kindreds, and</u>**

---

[154] Jeremiah 1:5 ...I ordained thee a prophet unto <u>the nations</u>.
Acts 9:15 But the Lord said unto him, Go thy way: for he is a chosen vessel unto me, to bear my name before <u>the Gentiles</u>, and kings, and the children of Israel:
[155] Revelation 14:4 These are they which were <u>not defiled with women</u>; for they are <u>virgins.</u>
[156] Revelation 14:3 And they sung as it were a new song before the throne... and no man could learn that song but <u>the hundred *and* forty *and* four thousand</u>, which were <u>redeemed</u> from the earth.
[157] Matthew 22:3 And sent forth his servants to call them that were bidden to the wedding: <u>and they would not come.</u>
[158] Matthew 24:9 Then shall they deliver you up to be <u>afflicted</u>, and shall <u>kill</u> you: and ye shall be <u>hated</u> of all nations for my name's sake.
[159] Acts 1:8

people, and tongues (those are GENTILES)**, stood before the throne, and before the Lamb, clothed with white robes, and palms in their hands;**
v.10 And cried with a loud voice, saying, Salvation to our God which sitteth upon the throne, and unto the Lamb...
v.13 And one of the elders answered, saying unto me, <u>What are these which are arrayed in white robes? and whence came they?</u>
v.14 And I said unto him, Sir, thou knowest. And he said to me, <u>These are they which came out of great tribulation</u>, and have washed their robes, and made them white in the blood of the Lamb.

These are Gentiles who were converted by the preaching of the 144,000 and died sometime during the last 3 ½ years of the Time of the End (the Great Tribulation). It is likely that these multitudes are mostly ex-Muslims who lived in countries that were closed to the Gospel and foreign missionaries during the Church Age. Paul said in his second epistle to the Thessalonians that God was going to send strong delusion for the purpose of damnation upon all those who received not the love of the truth (the Gospel)[160]. Since most of the first-world and even second-world countries have had the Gospel for centuries, it is probable that they will be the ones who receive that **"strong delusion"** from God.

It does not appear that these End Time Gentile converts get raptured up to heaven, but rather that they are killed or die upon the earth shortly after the final 3 ½ years begin. They may have met their fate by being executed for their faith, by starvation for not receiving the mark of the Beast, or as a consequence of the trumpet or vial judgments, but regardless, they wind up in Heaven where they hunger no more and **"God shall wipe away all tears from their eyes"**[161].

This final Gentile revival marks the time when **"the fullness of**

---

[160] **2 Thessalonians 2:10-12**
[161] Revelation 7:16 **They shall <u>hunger no more, neither thirst any more</u>; neither shall the sun light on them, nor any heat.**
v.17 For the Lamb which is in the midst of the throne shall feed them, and shall lead them unto living fountains of waters: <u>and God shall wipe away all tears from their eyes.</u>

the Gentiles be come in"[162]. The fullness of the Gentiles does <u>not</u> come in and is not fulfilled at the rapture of the Church because 1) There is still another huge group of End Time Gentiles that still have to yet to come in and 2) This **"fullness of the Gentiles"** corresponds to the awakening of Israel[163], which does NOT happen at the rapture of the Church, but rather around the start of the Great Tribulation![164]

As for the 144,000 themselves, the calling and sealing of these servants occurs toward the very beginning of the 10 year Time of the End. In Revelation chapter 7, the Scriptures give a major clue as to the TIMING of their calling: when they are called and sealed, <u>the earth has not been harmed yet.</u>

Revelation 7:1 And after these things I saw four angels standing on the four corners of the earth, holding the four winds of the earth, that the wind should not blow on the earth, nor on the sea, nor on any tree.

v.2 And I saw another angel ascending from the east, having the seal of the living God: and he cried with a loud voice to the four angels, to whom it was given to hurt the earth and the sea,

v.3 Saying, <u>Hurt not the earth, neither the sea, nor the trees, TILL we have sealed the servants of our God in their foreheads.</u>

The 7 trumpet judgments, the 7 vial judgments and seal judgments #4,5,6 and 7 occur during **"the Great Tribulation"** (the last 3 ½ years). The White Horse, Red Horse and Black Horse (Seals #1,2 and 3) occur during this 7 year **"Beginning of Sorrows"**, and the Pale Horse corresponds to the resurrection of the Antichrist (Satan's Advent) at the start of the Great Tribulation. The 144,000 <u>have</u> to be sealed <u>before the Red Horseman</u> shows up because he **"takes peace from <u>the earth</u>"**[165], and the 144,000 must be sealed BEFORE anything happens to <u>the earth</u>.

---

[162] **Romans 11:25**

[163] **Romans 11:25 For I would not, brethren, that ye should be ignorant of this mystery, lest ye should be wise in your own conceits; that <u>blindness in part is happened to Israel, UNTIL the fulness of the Gentiles be come in.</u>**

[164] Therefore the idea that Jesus is waiting to come back until the last person on His pre-ordained list gets saved is nonsense and the Church rapture has NOTHING to do with Paul's statement of **"until the fullness of the Gentiles be come in"**.

[165] **Revelation 6:4**

As was stated before, once Satan's Advent is located on the prophetic timeline, all other prophetic events can begin to be sorted out chronologically. The Pale Horse is ridden by an ENTITY whose name is Death and Hell. Whereas this entity is not necessarily Satan or the Antichrist himself, Death and Hell do closely correspond with Satan and his activities, and it is no stretch of the imagination to say that this Pale Horseman begins his ride at the moment the Antichrist rises from the dead; for **"THEN shall be great tribulation"**[166] and this Pale Horseman has the awesome power to kill with sword, hunger, death and the beasts of the earth on a worldwide scale. Seeing as how this 4th horseman corresponds to the beginning of the final 3 ½ years, it is therefore obvious that the first three horsemen ride during the first 7 years of the Time of the End (the time of the Beginning of Sorrows), which also places the sealing of the 144,000 prior to the 2nd Horseman, toward the very beginning of the Time of the End.

The Devil is going to select his servant (the Antichrist) toward the end of the Church Age[167], and at the very start of the 10 year Time of the End he commissions him with a "ministry" to go forth **"conquering and to conquer"**. This is probably Satan's counter-move to the Lord's calling and commissioning of the 144,000, which also takes place toward the start of the Time of the End. The 144,000 are special apostles who are given the dirty work of preaching to the multitudes of the Earth that will be living during the End Times, so it certainly stands to reason that their calling and sealing would occur toward the beginning of the Time of the End, very closely following the rapture of the Church. In fact, the sealing of the 144,000 might even be SIMUTANEOUS with the rapture of the Church.

A peculiar order of events is given in **Acts 8-9** in which there is an Ethiopian eunuch who gets saved after hearing a Church Age Gospel from a Church Age preacher, and the Ethiopian becomes a Church Age Christian. Then, *for some odd reason,* the Holy Spirit pulls Philip up into the air and transports him supernaturally! What

---

[166] **Matthew 24:21**

[167] The man of sin will be recognized by discerning Christians just prior to the Church's rapture according to **2 Thessalonians 2:3.**

84

was the POINT in that?! It is so strikingly out of the ordinary that it demands everyone's attention! In Acts chapter 8, we have what appears to be a TYPE of the Church Age rapture. Then, lo and behold, in the very next chapter, the scene switches to a MALE JEWISH VIRGIN who is an ENEMY of the Church[168]. He SEES the Lord IN THE AIR and HEARS A VOICE (!). He instantly becomes converted, and shortly thereafter his personal BLINDNESS goes away[169]. Judging by the order of events in Acts 8-9, the salvation of Saul (Paul) seems to occur very shortly after Philip's "rapture", possibly even at the same instant. I suspect that when the Church MEETS the Lord in the air, 144,000 unsaved Jews will simultaneously SEE him in the air and HEAR his voice! This supernatural SIGN is the catalyst of their conversion and they are SEALED at that moment. Furthermore, because they SAW THE LORD, they fit the criteria to be APOSTLES[170] and consequently, the ability to perform SIGNS and MIRACLES is back, just as it was in the days of Jesus with his disciples[171]. Signs are for the JEWISH people [172] to whom the 144,000 are primarily sent to; however, at that time, the nation of Israel as a whole is still not ready to receive this "Gospel of the Kingdom"[173]. They will initially reject the preaching of the 144,000 and instead persecute them which will cause the 144,000 to direct their attention to the Gentiles who will then be converted by the THOUSANDS.

The rejection of the preaching of the 144,000 is prophesied by Jesus in **Matthew 24**, and notice that their preaching is during the time gap between the Church's rapture and Satan's Advent:
Matthew 24:3 ...Tell us, when shall these things be? and what *shall be* **the sign of thy coming, and of the end of the world?**

---

[168] Romans 11:28 As concerning the gospel, *they* (the Jews) *are* enemies for your sakes: but as touching the election, *they are* beloved for the fathers' sakes.
[169] Romans 11:25 For I would not, brethren, that ye should be ignorant of this mystery, lest ye should be wise in your own conceits; that blindness in part is happened to Israel, until the fulness of the Gentiles be come in.
[170] 1 Corinthians 9:1 Am I not an apostle? am I not free? have I not SEEN Jesus Christ our Lord?....
[171] Signs and Miracles will be in vogue during the End Times: **Hebrews 6:4-5, Romans 15:19, 2 Corinthians 12:12, Mark 16:17-18, James 5:14 + Mark 6:13**
[172] 1 Corinthians 1:22 For the Jews require a sign....
[173] NOT the Gospel of the grace of God that we preach during the Church Age.

v.4 And Jesus answered and said unto them, Take heed that no man deceive you.

SEAL #1: WHITE HORSE (Antichrist)

v.5 For many shall come in my name, saying, <u>I am Christ</u>; and shall deceive many.

SEAL #2: RED HORSE (War)

v.6-7 And ye shall hear of wars and rumours of wars: see that ye be not troubled: for all *these things* must come to pass, but the end is not yet. ("the end" is in **v.15** and is the final 3 ½ year Great Tribulation) **For <u>nation shall rise against nation</u>, and <u>kingdom against kingdom</u>....**

SEAL #3: BLACK HORSE (Famine)

v.7-8...and there shall be <u>famines</u>, and pestilences, and earthquakes, in divers places. All these *are* the beginning of sorrows.

INFORMATION ABOUT THE 144,000

v.9 Then shall they deliver you up to be afflicted, and shall kill you: and ye shall be hated of all nations for my name's sake.

Bear in mind that the Lord is speaking to his DISCIPLES here, <u>not</u> the Jewish race as a whole. Eventually, the entire world will turn against the Jewish race, but that does not happen until after Satan's Advent at the start of the Great Tribulation[174]. The future persecution that Jesus is referring to in verse 9 is the JEWISH PEOPLE persecuting their JEWISH PREACHERS (the 144,000). The 144,000 will be hated <u>by their own people</u> (like Paul and Jeremiah were) and hated by the rest of the world.

Pay close attention and notice that these events are happening AFTER the Church has been raptured. Granted, the Body of Christ in the last days of the Church Age could 'catch a whiff' of the 'fumes' of the Time of the End and see wars, famines and

---

[174] **Revelation 13:7 And it was given unto him to make war with the saints, and to overcome them: and power was given him over all kindreds, and tongues, and nations.** This does not happen until AFTER the Antichrist rises from the dead.

pestilences, but the actual <u>context</u> of these verses is POST-CHURCH RAPTURE. This is evident by the fact that these preachers are preaching a GOSPEL OF THE KINGDOM OF HEAVEN message and enduring to the end is a CONDITION of salvation at that time:

v.13 But he that shall <u>endure unto the end</u>, the same shall be saved.[175]

v.14 And this gospel of the <u>kingdom</u>[176] shall be preached in all the world for a witness unto all nations; and then shall <u>THE END</u> come.

Pay attention to that phrase **"the end"** because it can have multiple applications in the context of the last days:

- It can presumably refer to THE END of a saint's life (he endured and was martyred)[177].
- It can refer to THE END of the Great Tribulation period (i.e. 2nd Advent)[178].
- It can refer to the entire 3 ½ year Great Tribulation time period, which is THE END of the current world system[179].

SEAL #4: PALE HORSE & "THE END"

v.15 When ye therefore shall see the abomination of desolation.....stand in the holy place.....

Since the Church HAS to be raptured out prior to **v.3-14** and **v.15-28** describe the final 3 ½ years of the Great Tribulation, it is clear that **v.3-14** are describing the things that will occur during the TIME GAP between the Church's rapture and Satan's Advent. It is important to understand that it is during this 7 year time gap that the 144,000 will be commissioned to preach to the Jews first, but

---

[175] NOT a Church Age Doctrine!

[176] NOT a Church Age Gospel!

[177] **John 13:1 ...when Jesus knew that his hour was come that he should depart out of this world unto the Father, having loved his own which were in the world, he loved them unto <u>the end</u>.**

[178] **Matthew 13:40 As therefore the tares are gathered and burned in the fire; so shall it be <u>in the end</u> of this world.**

[179] **Daniel 12:6 And *one* said to the man clothed in linen, which *was* upon the waters of the river, How long *shall it be to* <u>the end</u> of these wonders?**
v.7 And I heard the man clothed in linen...that *it shall be* <u>for a time, times, and an half</u>; and when he shall have accomplished to scatter the power of the holy people, all these *things* shall be finished.

will be rejected and persecuted by them. Having this understanding will help you to interpret the chronology and placement of events in some of the more difficult passages, such as **Matthew 22:**

v.1 And Jesus answered and spake unto them again by parables, and said,

v.2 The <u>kingdom of heaven</u> is like unto a certain king, which made a MARRIAGE for his son,

v.3 And sent forth his SERVANTS to call them that were bidden (The Jews; the Nation of Israel) **to the WEDDING: and they would not come.**

Pay attention that this is a KINGDOM OF HEAVEN passage and therefore has absolutely NOTHING to do (doctrinally) with the Church Age! This is a very crucial detail because what follows is an END TIMES passage that involves a bunch of SERVANTS (not SONS![180]) who are bidding people to be GUESTS (not the BRIDE!) at a WEDDING and partake of a FEAST thereat (not to GET MARRIED)! The **"servants"** are most likely the 144,000 according to **Revelation 7:3**[181].

v.4 Again, he sent forth other <u>servants</u>, saying, Tell them which are bidden (Jews), **Behold, I have prepared my DINNER: my oxen and _my_ fatlings _are_ killed, and all things _are_ ready: <u>come unto the marriage.</u>**

Notice that the invitation is not to MARRY the Son but to be a GUEST at the wedding FEAST. In the Old Testament, it was common for a marriage to be followed by a feast[182], which is exactly what we have here in this passage. In regard to future prophecy, the ESPOUSED[183] Bride of Christ (the Church) becomes MARRIED at the <u>moment</u> her Lord comes for her at the rapture. The marriage is, in a sense, "consummated" in that moment because the Bride enters into the CHAMBER with her husband and they are no longer just ONE SPIRIT[184] but they are

---

[180] The 144,000 are called **"servants"** in **Revelation 7:3**, and are NEVER called "sons".

[181] **Revelation 7:3 Saying, Hurt not the earth, neither the sea, nor the trees, till we have sealed <u>the servants</u> of our God in their foreheads.**

[182] Jacob: **Genesis 29:21-28,** Samson: **Judges 14:8-11,** Ahasuerus: **Esther 2:17-18**

[183] **2 Corinthians 11:2 For I am jealous over you with godly jealousy: for I have <u>espoused</u> you to one husband, that I may present _you as_ a chaste virgin to Christ.**

[184] **1 Corinthians 6:17 But he that is joined unto the Lord is <u>one spirit.</u>**

now also ONE FLESH[185], which is the Biblical definition of marriage[186]. At the rapture, our FLESH is made just like His FLESH, just as Eve's flesh was like Adam's flesh. Notice in **Genesis 2:23** that Adam and Eve were one flesh WITHOUT any sexual act occurring. This is unique to Adam and Eve and is a picture of the Lord Jesus Christ and His bride. Jesus Christ and the Church, at the time of the rapture, can legitimately be classified as **"one flesh"**, not only because they will have similar glorified bodies, but because everything about the Church's life and existence at that time will be *by, in, through, from*, and *because of* Jesus Christ, just as Eve's life and existence was *by, in, through, from*, and *because of* Adam.

While the Bride is being rewarded and adorned at the Judgment Seat of Christ[187], the Father commissions 144,000 Jews to go out and round up some guests for His Son's WEDDING FEAST that is soon to commence in Heaven[188]. The Jews missed out on the MARRIAGE (first rapture) but they still have a chance to get in on the FEAST (second rapture).

v.5 But they (the Jews) **made light of *it,* and went their ways, one to his farm, another to his merchandise:**

---

[185] **Genesis 2:22 ...he** (the Lord God)**...brought her** (the Church) **unto the man** (Jesus Christ). **And Adam said, <u>This is now bone of my bones, and flesh of my flesh</u>....
1 John 3:2 ... but we know that, when he shall appear, we shall be like him** (physically) **for we shall see him as he is.**
[186] P.S. There is not any kind of weird sensuality that takes place at this time.
[187] Not whipped! The only "suffering" at the Judgment Seat of Christ is the suffering of **"LOSS"** (**1 Corinthians 3:15**). The passage used to prove a whipping is in **Luke 12:47-48** which has NOTHING AT ALL to do with Church Age Christians. Also, where will you find a cross reference of a wife being WHIPPED by her husband in the Bible?
[188] **Matthew 22** is not a MILLENNIUM passage, and saying that the Marriage Feast is on the earth at the beginning of the Millennium will not work either because:
#1. The Kingdom of Heaven is not just limited to the actual Millennium but can apply to the time immediately preceding it (**Matthew 3:2**)
#2. This passage would then imply that there will be some <u>Jews</u> who refuse to go to Jerusalem at the start of the Millennium, which is inconsistent with **Matthew 24:31, Isaiah 11:11-12, 43:5-7,** and **Psalm 50:5**
#3. For a bunch of Jews to be concerned with their "farming" and "merchandise" after 3 ½ years of racial genocide by Satan is a bit of a stretch, is it not?
#4. This passage would then be saying that some of King Jesus' messengers are being KILLED by JEWS during the Millennium!! **v.6**
#5. King Jesus would then be going around burning up <u>Jewish</u> cities <u>in Israel</u> during the Millennium!! **v.7**

v.6 And the remnant took his servants (144,000)**, and entreated** *them* **spitefully, and slew** *them.*

v.7 But when the king heard *thereof,* **he was wroth: and he sent forth his armies, and destroyed those murderers, and burned up their city.**[189]

v.8 Then saith he to his servants, The wedding is ready, but they which were bidden (nation of Israel) **were not worthy**.

The <u>nation</u> of Israel does not 'wake up' at the rapture of the Church, even if there *ARE* airplanes falling from the sky, driverless cars crashing everywhere, and 90% of America's population is missing[190]. The <u>nation of Israel</u> will not begin to turn back to God until they are AFFLICTED[191] which Biblically does not happen until the Great Tribulation[192]. As a matter of fact, for the first 7 years after the rapture of the Church, Israel will be going about her business as usual:

Matthew 22:5 But they made light of it (the preaching of the 144,000)**, and went their ways, one to his farm, another to his merchandise.**

Even after millions (?) of people suddenly disappear and all of the calamities resulting from that, the Jews will quickly go back to

---

[189] This CANNOT be 70 AD (due to Kingdom of Heaven context), this CANNOT be during the Church Age (due to Kingdom of Heaven context) and this CANNOT be the 2nd Advent because the city is evidently Jerusalem and Jesus SAVES Jerusalem at the 2nd Advent, not DESTROYS it! So this burning of the city must happen sometime during the Beginning of Sorrows. It looks like this is a major future attack on Jerusalem by IRAN (**Isaiah 22:1-14, 21:1-5, 42:24-25**; probably connected with the White Horse) which ignites World War 3 (Red Horse) and results in UN security forces surrounding Jerusalem (**Luke 21:20**) trying to maintain a cease fire. During the battle, the city of Jerusalem was **"burned up"**, but not completely destroyed. It can be speculated that the Dome of the Rock is destroyed, and since the Jews were not the aggressors, they win the right to rebuild their Temple on the Temple Mount.

The **"King"** in the passage is certainly the Lord, and He sends **"HIS armies"**, but it should be remembered that God has often claimed a foreign, Gentile army tasked with punishing His people as His OWN ARMY: **Jeremiah 25:9, Psalm 17:13, Mark 12:9, 2 Chronicles 36:17, Lamentations 1:15, 2:5-9, Amos 3:6, Isaiah 29:3**

[190] LOL – *yah right!*

[191] **Hosea 5:15 I will go** *and* **return to my place, till they acknowledge their offence, and seek my face: <u>in their affliction they will seek me early.</u>**

[192] Of course, the Jewish people have been 'afflicted' for the last 2,000 years, but it is going to take more than concentration camps and crematoriums to wake them up. The **"affliction"** that God has in mind is going to be at the hand of Satan incarnate which will be like nothing the world has ever seen.

90

business as usual and will continue to mess around with their worldly possessions and money-making operations, and evidently will not be too concerned or worried about anything that has occurred.

v.9 Go ye therefore into the highways, and as many as ye shall find, bid to the marriage (i.e. to the marriage FEAST, not to BE MARRIED to the bridegroom).

v.10 So those servants went out into the highways, and gathered together all as many as they found, both bad and good: and the wedding was furnished with GUESTS.[193]

GUESTS; not a bride; not sons and daughters; not servants; GUESTS![194]

Look at it again in **Luke 12:**

v.35 Let your loins be girded about, and *your* lights burning;
The idea of being alert and having a burning light or a lamp or a candlestick is something that will show up over and over in this Beginning of Sorrows context.

v.36 And ye yourselves like unto men that wait for their lord, when he will <u>return from the wedding</u>....
Notice that he is RETURNING from the wedding; He has ALREADY married his bride, therefore the people that He is coming for CANNOT be Church Age Christians, and this CANNOT be a Church Age passage.

...that when he cometh and knocketh, they may open unto him immediately.
Here we have the **"door"** showing up again: that DOOR is up in the 2nd heaven and is the entrance into, and out of, the 3rd heaven;

---

[193] The **"bad"** out in the **"highways"** and **"streets and lanes of the city"** are probably not Gentiles, but rather the **"poor, and the maimed, and the halt, and the blind"** (**Luke 14:21**) as Luke's account interprets them to be. It would make sense for the 144,000 to go after them seeing as they are who Jesus went after in the Gospels. Those out in the **"highways and hedges"** are probably Jews outside of Judea, possibly like the Samarian woman and maniac of Gadera.

[194] Verses 2-10 are BEFORE the 2nd Advent, during the Time of the End; verses 11-14 are AFTER the 2nd Advent, around the beginning of the Millennium.

like a 'STARGATE' so to speak[195]. When John saw that door open up in the 2nd heaven, he was immediately transported into the 3rd heaven (**Revelation 4:1**). This KNOCKING at the door and sudden appearance of Jesus Christ is what the Jews are to be WATCHING for during the time of the Beginning of Sorrows. The Scripture warns them to open to him **"IMMEDIATELY"**, and those who DO will be rewarded:

v.37 Blessed *are* those <u>servants</u> (not SONS), whom the lord when he cometh shall find WATCHING: verily I say unto you, that he shall gird himself, and make them to <u>sit down to meat</u>, and will come forth and serve them.

They are taken through the DOOR to a FEAST in HEAVEN that happens after a WEDDING has occurred, and <u>by getting in on this FEAST they 'skip out' on the Great Tribulation Period!</u>

Do you see now why it is <u>so important</u> that they WATCH?

Do you see now why this concept is repeated over and over and OVER, particularly in the <u>Kingdom of Heaven</u> gospels (Matthew, Mark and Luke)?

v.38 And if he shall come in the second watch (midnight)**, or come in the third watch** (cock-crowing)**, and find *them* so, blessed are those servants.**

The rapture of the Church is at the <u>start</u> of the EVENING watch (6:00 pm), the 2nd Advent occurs that the <u>end</u> of the MORNING watch (6:00 am), and the conditional rapture of the Jewish saints who are WATCHING occurs sometime during the MIDNIGHT watch (9:00 pm – 12:00 am). The ones who are obedient and are watching are said to be **"blessed"**, and are **"better"** off according to **Proverbs 25:7**[196]. Indeed, being absent for the worst time period the earth has ever seen is certainly a 'blessing'[197]!

Matthew 25:1 Then shall the <u>kingdom of heaven</u> (NOT a Church Age passage) **be likened unto TEN virgins, which took**

---

[195] **1 Kings 6:8** gives more information on the structure and workings of the universe than all of the knowledge of NASA, Albert Einstein, Steven Hawking and CERN combined.

[196] **Proverbs 25:7 For <u>better</u> *it is* that it be said unto thee, Come up hither; than that thou shouldest be put lower in the presence of the prince whom thine eyes have seen.**

[197] **Revelation 16:15, Luke 12:37, Matthew 24:46, Luke 14:15 (Daniel 12:12 ?)**

their lamps, and went forth to meet the bridegroom.

Why 10 virgins?

Why not 7 virgins?

Why not 3 ½ virgins?

According to **Revelation 7** these virgins are Jewish MALES who are preparing to MEET the Bridegroom, not MARRY him.

v.2 And five of them were wise, and five *were* foolish.

v.3 They that *were* foolish took their LAMPS, and took no OIL with them:

The two elements mentioned are LIGHT and OIL. Many commentators suggest that the oil is a type of the Holy Spirit that has been lost and as a consequence, these foolish virgins are now going to be left behind at the rapture of the Church.

Nothing could be further from the truth.

First of all, the passage has absolutely nothing to do with born again Christians in the Church Age, and therefore the rapture in the passage cannot possibly be the Church Age rapture!

Second, oil being a type of the Holy Spirit is not the only possible interpretation, for oil is also sometimes likened to PRAYER. In **1 Samuel 10:1**, Samuel is pouring a VIAL of anointing OIL on Saul's head. This is the first mention of the word **"vial"** in the Bible and it is connected with OIL. This is important to notice because the first mention of a word in the Bible almost always sets the precedent for how it will usually be used throughout the rest of the Bible. In the fifth chapter of the book of Revelation, there are some VIALS that are filled with **"odours"** which are said to be **"the prayers of saints"** [198]. There are two things in the Bible that can give a sweet **"odour"** and they are SPICES and OILS, so the question is: are the vials filled with SPICE (solid) or OIL (liquid)?

Revelation 8:3 And another angel came and stood at the altar, having a golden censer; and there was given unto him much <u>incense</u> (spice), that he should offer *it* <u>WITH the prayers of all saints</u> (oil) upon the golden altar which was before the throne.

v.4 And the smoke of the incense (spice), *which came* <u>WITH</u>

---

[198] Revelation 5:8 And when he had taken the book, the four beasts and four *and* twenty elders fell down before the Lamb, having every one of them harps, and golden <u>vials full of odours</u>, which are the prayers of saints.

the prayers of the saints (oil), ascended up before God out of the angel's hand.

Be careful to notice that the prayers are offered WITH the incense (spice), but the prayers are evidently not the incense itself. The incense is the SPICE and the PRAYERS could be the OIL. Putting chapter 5 and chapter 8 together, it is apparent that the OILS are the PRAYERS of the saints which are contained in vials in chapter 5 and are offered with the spice of the incense in chapter 8. Once the vials are emptied of the first liquid (OIL), they are then refilled with another liquid: WINE[199].

The OIL in **Matthew 25** is a type of PRAYER (not a type of the Holy Spirit), and the LIGHT speaks of visibility or WATCHFULLNESS in the NIGHT, thus making **Matthew 25** perfectly consistent with all of the other passages in Matthew, Mark and Luke that tell the End Times saints to **"WATCH (lamp / light) and PRAY (oil)"**!

v.4 But the wise took oil in their vessels with their lamps.

They need these metaphorical LAMPS because it is metaphorically NIGHT TIME. Don't forget: night time is likened to the Time of the End, NOT the Church Age as far as God's prophetic time clock is concerned. There are some similarities and applicable types between the Church Age and night time, such as the Church being a type of the moon reflecting the light of the Sun upon a darkened earth, but this type cannot speak of the prophetic **"times and seasons"**[200] ('dispensation', if you will) because the Church Age lasts for nearly 2,000 years which is two full days and two full nights according to the 1,000 year = 1 day equation given in **2 Peter 3:8**. For the "Church Age = Night Time" theory to be consistent, it would require roughly 500 years to be 'day time', then 500 years to be 'night time', then 500 years to be 'day time', the 500 years to be 'night time'; which is interesting, but does not match the events of Church history at all. Yes, **Romans 13:12** talks about the **"night"** being **"far spent"** and **"the day"** being **"at hand"**, but it is obvious from the passage that a dispensational

---

[199] **Revelation 15:7, 19**
[200] **1 Thessalonians 5:1**

time frame is NOT what is being alluded to, but rather a SPIRITUAL comparison between the old carnal life of the **"works of darkness"** and the new Christian life of the **"armour of light"**. If this was not enough, Paul goes even further and tells the Thessalonian Christians that we are **"children of LIGHT, and children of THE DAY"** and **"we are NOT of the night, nor of darkness"**[201]! In regard to 'dispensations', the "Church Age = Night Time" theory does not work, but the "Time of the End = Night Time" theory does.

v.5 While the bridegroom tarried, they all slumbered and slept.
   They are sleeping because it is NIGHT TIME.
 v.6 And at <u>MIDNIGHT</u> there was a cry made, Behold, the bridegroom cometh; go ye out to <u>meet</u> him.
v.7 Then all those virgins arose, and trimmed their lamps.
v.8 And the foolish said unto the wise, Give us of your oil; for our lamps are gone out.
v.9 But the wise answered, saying, *Not so;* lest there be not enough for us and you: but go ye rather to them that sell, and buy for yourselves.
v.10 And while they went to buy, the bridegroom came; and they that were ready <u>went in with him to the MARRIAGE</u>: and the DOOR was shut.

   This is absolutely a RAPTURE: someone is PHYSICALLY leaving the world through a DOOR in the sky just like John did when he was raptured[202]! What is the DOCTRINAL explanation of this passage though? This CANNOT be the Church Age rapture, otherwise one would have to concede that the rapture of the Church is <u>conditional</u> and some Christians <u>can</u> be left behind! Also, this CANNOT be the rapture that happens toward the END of the Great Tribulation period, because this rapture in **Matthew 25** involves LIVING people, not DEAD people, and, these raptured saints in **Matthew 25** are leaving the earth to get in on a <u>wedding feast</u> whereas the saints who are raptured toward the end

---

[201] 1 Thessalonians 5:5
[202] Revelation 4:1

of the Great Tribulation period are taken up to prepare for imminent battle (Armageddon).

I contend that **Matthew 25:1-13** speaks of a conditional rapture of Jewish End Times saints and occurs sometime during **"the beginning of sorrows"** which is between the rapture of the Church and the start of the GREAT Tribulation (final 3 ½ years). Watchful Jews will go up and miss out on the Great Tribulation Period but the rest will be left behind and have to **"endure unto the end"**.

Here it is AGAIN:

Song of Solomon 5:1 (Jesus Christ speaking) **I am come into my garden, my sister, *my* spouse: I have gathered my myrrh with my spice; I have eaten my honeycomb with my honey; I have drunk my wine with my milk: EAT, O <u>FRIENDS</u>; drink, yea, drink abundantly, O beloved.**

Here in the passage the Lord is eating some food and invites his beloved FRIENDS to join Him. Here is what his 'beloved friends' (the Jews[203]) have to say:

v.2 I SLEEP (Oh boy, this does not sound good, especially with those slumbering virgins in mind!) **but my heart waketh: *it is* the voice of my beloved that KNOCKETH** (there is that DOOR again!)**, *saying,* Open to me, my sister, my love, my dove, my undefiled: for my head is filled with dew, *and* my locks with the drops of the NIGHT** (Time of the End)**.**

Now admittedly, the references to **"my dove"** and **"my undefiled"** certainly point to the Bride of Christ (the Church), but if the CHURCH is indeed the woman in this passage, then it will be very hard to explain why she is LEFT BEHIND in the following verses!

Song of Solomon is tough like that: sometimes it sounds like the woman is the CHURCH and sometimes it sounds like the woman is ISRAEL. Sometimes it is hard to tell if Solomon is talking about Pharaoh's daughter[204] (CHURCH) or Abishag[205] (ISRAEL). Is the

---

[203] **Romans 11:28 As concerning the gospel, *they are* enemies for your sakes: but as touching the election, *<u>they are</u>* <u>beloved</u> for the fathers' sakes.**

[204] **1 Kings 3:1 And Solomon made affinity with Pharaoh king of Egypt, and <u>took Pharaoh's daughter</u>, and brought her into the city of David...**

woman a Shulamite[206] (ISRAEL) or an Egyptian[207] (CHURCH)? Her identity is somewhat MYSTERIOUS[208], wouldn't you say? It seems to FLIP BACK AND FORTH (depending on the context) almost as though there are TWO WOMEN that are both important to the Lord! Kind of like David (type: Jesus Christ) who married **Abigail** whose name means "my FATHER is joy" (ISRAEL) <u>AND</u> **Ahinoam** whose name means "my BROTHER is my delight" (CHURCH)!!![209] So one could make an argument for either side and oftentimes the Lord is not as 'cut and dry' as we would prefer Him to be. The safest route is to acknowledge that the Lord greatly loves BOTH women (ISRAEL and the CHURCH) and that the Song of Solomon has SOME practical application to the Church and SOME doctrinal application to Israel and that the reader has to discern what goes where and to whom <u>by comparing Scripture with Scripture</u>. It makes the most sense to say that Song of Solomon chapter 5 has some PRACTICAL insights for the Church, but it applies DOCTRINALLY to Jewish End Times saints, specifically during the time of **"the Beginning of Sorrows"**.

v.3 I have put off my coat; how shall I put it on? I have washed my feet; how shall I defile them?
  Notice that her EXCUSES[210] cause her to HESITATE and not open to him IMMEDIATELY[211].
v.4 My beloved put in his hand by the hole of _THE DOOR_ (!), and my bowels were moved for him.
v.5 I rose up to open to my beloved; and my hands dropped

---

[205] **1 Kings 1:3 So they sought for a fair damsel throughout all the coasts of Israel, and found <u>Abishag a Shunammite</u>, and brought her to the king.** Solomon is very JEALOUS for her in **ch.2:21-24**, so much so that he KILLS Adonijah for going after her. This jealousy is unfounded unless Solomon himself intended to marry her.
[206] **Song of Solomon 6:13 Return, return, O <u>Shulamite</u>...**
[207] **Song of Solomon 1:5 I am <u>black</u>, but comely, O ye daughters of Jerusalem...**
[208] **Ephesians 5:32 This is a great <u>mystery</u>: but I speak concerning <u>Christ and the church.</u>**
[209] 1 Samuel 25:42-43
[210] **Luke 14:16 ...A certain man made a great SUPPER and bade many....**
v.18 And they all with one consent began to make <u>EXCUSE</u>....
[211] **Luke 12:36 And ye yourselves like unto men that wait for their lord, when he will return from the wedding; that when he cometh and <u>knocketh</u>, they may <u>open unto him IMMEDIATELY.</u>**

97

with __myrrh__, **and my fingers** *with* **sweet smelling** __myrrh__, **upon the handles of the lock.**

Pay attention to that little detail about the "myrrh", that will be an important clue later on.

v.6 I opened to my beloved; __but my beloved had withdrawn__ __himself,__ *__and was gone__* __....__

WHY? Answer: **...my soul FAILED when he spake....**

And what an EPIC FAIL this is! Her <u>one chance</u> to avoid the coming Great Tribulation period, and she blew it! The Lord advises in **Isaiah 26:20 "Come, my people** (Jews)**, enter thou into thy CHAMBERS** (Heaven)**, and shut thy DOORS** (Heaven) **about thee: hide thyself as it were for a little moment** (in Heaven)**,** __until the INDIGNATION be overpast__ (Great Tribulation period)**."**

She was told over and over to WATCH and PRAY (i.e. be ready for His appearance) but she FAILED, and as a consequence, she starts having some serious trouble:

....I sought him, but I could not find him; I called him, but he gave me no answer.

The Lord is hiding His face from her now. The door is SHUT. Remember how the parable in **Matthew 25** ends?

Matthew 25:10 And while they went to buy, the bridegroom came; and they that were READY went in with him to the marriage (the marriage feast <u>in heaven</u>)**: and the DOOR was SHUT.**

v.11 Afterward came also the other virgins, saying, Lord, __Lord, open to us__.

They are calling after him just like the woman in Song of Solomon did. In the Song of Solomon, the woman was given **"no answer"**, whereas these foolish virgins DO get an answer: **v.12 But he answered and said, Verily I say unto you, I know you not.** This apparent contradiction can be solved by taking Luke's version of the story into account:

Luke 13:25 When once the master of the house is risen up, and hath SHUT to THE DOOR, and ye begin to STAND WITHOUT, and to KNOCK at the door, saying, __Lord, Lord,__ __open unto us__**; and he shall answer and say unto you, I know you not whence ye are:**

v.26 Then shall ye begin to say, We have eaten and drunk in thy presence, and thou hast taught in our streets.

v.27 But he shall say, I tell you, I know you not whence ye are; depart from me, all *ye* workers of iniquity.

v.28 There shall be weeping and gnashing of teeth, when ye shall see Abraham, and Isaac, and Jacob, and all the prophets, in the kingdom of God, and you *yourselves* thrust out.

v.29 And they shall come from the east, and *from* the west, and from the north, and *from* the south, and shall sit down in the kingdom of God.

Perhaps the Lord pokes His head out of the door and rebukes them (I doubt it), but it is more likely that there is a length of time between this rapture and this rebuke. These Jews were BLIND and so they completely missed the Church rapture (pre-End Times); then they were FOOLISH and missed the second rapture (mid-End Times), and unless they are DEAD, they will miss the third rapture (post-End Times)! After they miss the second rapture, they will be stuck on the Earth and will meet Satan incarnate face to face. There will be a lot of crying and praying and weeping, but it will be too late, they missed their last chance to get out. Now their only hope is to **"endure unto the end"**[212] but most of them will not. They were supposed to be **"follow[ing] peace and holiness, without which no man shall SEE the Lord"**[213]. They should have been **"LOOKING diligently lest any man FAIL of the grace of God"** because now a **"root of bitterness"** is going to 'spring up and trouble them and thereby many of them will end up being DEFILED'[214] (loose quote). This bitterness will cause many of these believing Jews to fall away and join the enemy. They will **"begin to smite his fellowservants, and to eat and drink with the drunken"**[215]. By leaving the friendship of their Beloved and becoming friends with the world, they are called **"adulterers and**

---

[212] Matthew 24:13 But he that shall endure unto the end, the same shall be saved.

[213] Hebrews 12:14 Follow peace with all *men,* and holiness, without which no man shall see the Lord:

[214] Hebrews 12:15 Looking diligently lest any man fail of the grace of God; lest any root of bitterness springing up trouble *you,* and thereby many be defiled;

[215] Matthew 24:49 And shall begin to smite *his* fellowservants, and to eat and drink with the drunken;

adultresses" who know not that **"the friendship of the world is enmity with God"** and **"whosoever therefore will be a friend of the world is the ENEMY of God"**[216]. This friendship is likened to adultery which also makes them a **"fornicator, or profane person, as Esau, who for ONE MORSEL OF MEAT sold his birthright"**[217]. How ironic that they could have partaken of a FEAST in Heaven but instead settled for a MORSEL on Earth. Indeed, just as Esau **"found no place of repentance, though he sought it carefully with tears"** so they will cry and weep, but because they 'sold out' and BETRAYED their Beloved, the Bible says **"For ye know how that AFTERWARD, when he WOULD HAVE inherited the blessing, he was REJECTED"**[218].

   "Afterward" is the KEY WORD. **There is a space between the door being shut and the final answer of rejection[219].** The door shuts and the foolish virgins cry and beg, but He gives them **"no answer"**[220]. Out of bitterness against Jesus, these foolish VIRGINS become <u>ADULTERERS</u> and turn to the sweet Mother of <u>HARLOTS</u>, MYSTERY BABYLON, who receives them with open arms. They will inevitably take the mark of Beast (once it is made available after the Antichrist rises from the dead[221]) and partake of the dainty, deceitful meats[222] of **"the man that hath an evil eye"**[223]. Their Beloved invited them to eat and drink[224], but

---

[216] James 4:4 Ye adulterers and adulteresses, know ye not that the friendship of the world is enmity with God? whosoever therefore will be a friend of the world is the enemy of God.

[217] Hebrews 12:16 Lest there *be* any fornicator, or profane person, as Esau, who for one morsel of meat sold his birthright.

[218] Hebrews 12:17 For ye know how that afterward, when he would have inherited the blessing, he was rejected: for he found no place of repentance, though he sought it carefully with tears.

[219] This 'action - time gap - response' scenario is given again in **Luke 12:42-48.**

[220] Song of Solomon 5:6 ... I sought him, but I could not find him; I called him, but he gave me no answer.

[221] **Revelation 13:16-18** happens AFTER the Antichrist rises from the dead and therefore is only in effect during the final 3 ½ years of the Great Tribulation period.

[222] Proverbs 23:1 When thou sittest to eat with a <u>ruler,</u> consider diligently what *is* before thee...

v.3 Be not desirous of his <u>dainties</u>: for they *are* <u>deceitful meat.</u>

[223] Proverbs 23:6 Eat thou not the bread of *<u>him that hath</u> an evil eye*, neither desire thou his dainty meats:

[224] Song of Solomon 5:1 ...eat, O friends; drink, yea, drink abundantly, O beloved.

100

they refused Him. Now this new ruler extends the same invitation to **"eat and drink"**, except this man's heart is not with them[225]!

"AFTERWARD", that is, after the Time of the End is over and Jesus has returned, He will meet these traitorous Jews who will say to Him something to this effect: *"Hail master! Oh Jesus, remember us? We were your FRIENDS remember? We are so glad to finally see you!"*, but Jesus will say unto them, **"Verily I say unto you, I know you not (Matthew 25:12); I tell you, I know you not whence ye are; depart from me, all *ye* workers of iniquity (Luke 13:27)."** The Lord will then **"cut him asunder, and appoint *him* his portion with the hypocrites: there shall be weeping and gnashing of teeth."**

Song of Solomon 5:7 The watchmen that went about the city found me, they <u>smote me</u>, they <u>wounded me</u>; the keepers of the walls took away my veil from me.

There is some spiritual application that Church Age Christians can glean from this passage, but the DOCTRINAL application CANNOT at all apply to the Church. If this woman was the Bride of Christ, it would be awfully hard to explain the TRIBULATION that she experiences after missing her beloved at the DOOR! It is much more Biblically consistent to say that DOCTRINALLY this woman represents End Time Jews who miss out on a conditional rapture, and SPIRITUALLY she represents the Church whose selfish attitude causes her to miss out on daily fellowship with her beloved.

We now have four Bible texts that speak of this conditional rapture that will occur during **"the beginning of sorrows"**:
1) **Matthew 22**
2) **Luke 12**
3) **Matthew 25**
4) **Song of Solomon 5**

Now look at it played out in TYPE:
Matthew 26:36 Then cometh Jesus with them unto a place

---

[225] **Proverbs 25:7 For as he thinketh in his heart, so *is* he: <u>Eat and drink, saith he to thee; but his heart *is* not with thee.</u>**

called Gethsemane, and saith unto the disciples, Sit ye here, while I go and pray yonder.

v.37 And he took with him Peter and the two sons of Zebedee, and began to be SORROWFUL and very heavy.

This is a <u>time of sorrow</u> (!) here in the garden of Gethsemane. Jesus takes Peter, James and John with him into the garden, and after Jesus prays the first time, He returns and **"findeth them <u>ASLEEP</u>, and saith unto Peter, What, could ye not <u>watch</u> with me one hour?**

v.41 <u>WATCH and PRAY</u>…

Here we go again! Jesus gives the disciples the same exact command that is given to the Jews during the Time of the End! WHY should they watch and pray? That they **"enter not into temptation."** This obviously means that if they DO NOT watch and pray, they WILL enter into temptation!

…the spirit indeed *is* willing, but the flesh *is* weak.

This sounds a lot like the problem that the woman in the **Song of Solomon** had. Her BOWELS (insides / heart) were moved for her beloved, and eventually she dragged her lazy, sleepy, sorry, rear-end out of bed to open the door, but by then it was too late. Her SPIRIT was willing, but her FLESH was weak, and because her SOUL failed, her Beloved withdrew himself.

v.42 He went away again the second time, and prayed…..

v.43 And he came and found them <u>asleep</u> again: for their eyes were heavy.

They are <u>not</u> watching and are <u>not</u> praying. They probably had good intentions, but their flesh was weak, and according to Luke, they were **"sleeping for SORROW"**[226]!! The time in the Garden of Gethsemane is likened to the **"beginning of sorrows"** just as Calvary is a time of God's wrath being poured out and in that sense is a type of the **"Great Tribulation"**.

v.44 And he left them, and went away again, and prayed the third time, saying the same words.

The **"same words"** could be His prayer to the Father about the

---

[226] Luke 22:45 And when he rose up from prayer, and was come to his disciples, he found them <u>sleeping for sorrow</u>…

cup passing from Him, but the **"same words"** could also be a third admonition to Peter, James and John to watch and pray.

This whole scene starts with Jesus' command to **"tarry ye here and WATCH with me" (v.38)**. He then leaves, comes back, finds them asleep and reproves them the <u>first time</u> (Matthew and Mark's accounts). He then leaves again, comes back, finds them asleep again and reproves them the <u>second time</u> (Luke's account). He leaves a third time, comes back, again finds them asleep, and then gives his final, sad, <u>third statement</u> (Matthew and Mark's accounts):

v.45 Then cometh he to his disciples, and saith unto them, <u>Sleep on now, and take *your* rest:</u> behold, <u>THE HOUR</u> is at hand, and the Son of man is betrayed into the hands of sinners. v.46 Rise, let us be going: behold, he is at hand that doth betray me.

What is the **"hour"** that he is talking about? Well, He has only told them <u>3 times</u> that if they did not watch they would enter into **"temptation"**, so it is not a stretch to say that since they DID NOT watch, they are now facing **"THE HOUR"** of **"TEMPTATION"**. The "hour of temptation" is also directly connected to the Great Tribulation according to **Revelation 3:10**:

Because thou hast kept the word of my patience, I also will keep thee from <u>the hour of temptation</u>, which shall come upon all the world, to try them that dwell upon the earth.

...and look what happens during the **"hour of temptation"**: the Son of Perdition[227] comes!

v.47 And while he yet spake, lo, JUDAS, one of the twelve, came....

Judas (the Son of Perdition) shows up at the **"hour of temptation"** in Gethsemane, just as the Antichrist (the Son of Perdition) will show up at the **"hour of temptation"** during the Time of the End. The garden of Gethsemane incident is a TYPE or FORESHADOWING of the Time of the End scenario, except instead of Peter, James, John and Judas, the main characters are the End Time Jews and the Antichrist. When Judas Iscariot shows up in the garden of Gethsemane to betray Jesus, it is not only literal

---

[227] **John 17:12**

NIGHT TIME, but the Lord also commented that it was **"your hour, and the power of DARKNESS"**[228]; and just as God's Son, Jesus Christ, tasted the cup of the wrath of God on Calvary, God's son, Israel[229], will taste the cup of the wrath of God during the Great Tribulation.

If all of this was not enough, the Apostle Matthew incredibly gives us specific details as to the TIMING of these final events of Christ's life: at the last supper, Jesus told the disciples that one of the people in that room would betray him. Luke records that the disciples began to enquire who it was that Jesus was referring to but within moments questions became accusations and accusations became strife as to which of them was the greatest![230] While this bickering was taking place, Peter looked over at John, who was quietly lying on Jesus' chest and beckoned John to ask Jesus who the betrayer would be. John calmly inquired of Jesus **"who is it?"**, and Jesus whispered to John **"He it is, to whom I shall give a sop, when I have dipped it."**[231] It is evident that none of the other disciples heard Jesus say this because later when Judas left, they all assumed that he went out to feed the poor. John is the only disciple who knew ahead of time who the Son of Perdition was, and since John is a type of the Church, it stands to reason that at the end of the Church Age, Christians who are close to Jesus Christ will recognize who the Antichrist (Son of Perdition) is. This revelation will likely be brief and followed shortly by the rapture, for notice that Matthew states that it is EVENING (sometime between 6 pm - 9 pm) when this revelation takes place![232] After supper, they went to Gethsemane, where Jesus tells Peter, James and John to **"watch and pray"** while He prays separately to His Father. When He returns the first time and finds them sleeping, He rebukes Peter and says **"What, could ye not watch with me ONE HOUR?"**[233]. The obvious implication here is that He was away from them for ONE

---

[228] Luke22:53

[229] Exodus 4:22 And thou shalt say unto Pharaoh, Thus saith the LORD, Israel *is* my son, *even* my firstborn:

[230] Luke 13:21-24

[231] John 13:26

[232] Matthew 26:20 Now when the even was come, he sat down with the twelve.

[233] Matthew 26:40

HOUR, but what is not so obvious is that since He was away 3 separate times, he was presumably away for 3 hours. It is not a stretch of the imagination to say that they may have arrived to Gethsemane sometime after 9:00 pm which would put them into the MIDNIGHT WATCH (9 pm – 12 am), and this would mean that His earnest admonitions to **"watch and pray"** came during that Midnight watch, EXACTLY as it will for the End Time Jews who are also told to **"watch"**[234]! The disciples had 3 hours to watch and pray; they had the entire Midnight watch to obey the Lord, but they foolishly disobeyed and, coming suddenly, Jesus found them sleeping[235]. Immediately, Judas Iscariot, the Son of Perdition appears; but what TIME is it when he appears? It is very possible that he appears at the stroke of midnight, 12:00 am or shortly thereafter, which would match perfectly with the moment when **"the destroyer"**[236] (aka Abaddon, Appolyon[237]) came in the book of Exodus to kill the firstborn in the land of Egypt[238]. Whether Judas came at the stroke of midnight or shortly thereafter is debatable, but what is clear is that he came during the COCKCROWING watch (12:00 am – 3:00 am). This too is prophetically incredible when one considers that Satan's Advent and the start of the **"hour of temptation"** (3 ½ year Great Tribulation period) happens during the Cockcrowing watch of the prophetic night[239]! But it does not stop there: in chapter 27, Matthew records that Jesus was before the chief priests and

---

[234] Mark 13:37 And what I say unto you I say unto all, Watch.
[235] Mark 13:35 Watch ye therefore: for ye know not when the master of the house cometh, at even, or at midnight, or at the cockcrowing, or in the morning:
v.36 Lest coming suddenly he find you sleeping.
[236] Exodus 12:23 For the LORD will pass through to smite the Egyptians; and when he seeth the blood upon the lintel, and on the two side posts, the LORD will pass over the door, and will not suffer the destroyer to come in unto your houses to smite you.
[237] Revelation 9:11 And they had a king over them, *which is* the angel of the bottomless pit, whose name in the Hebrew tongue *is* Abaddon, but in the Greek tongue hath *his* name Apollyon.
[238] Exodus 11:4 And Moses said, Thus saith the LORD, About midnight will I go out into the midst of Egypt:
v.5 And all the firstborn in the land of Egypt shall die...
Exodus 12:29 And it came to pass, that at midnight the LORD smote all the firstborn in the land of Egypt...
[239] See Chart 6 on p. 128

delivered to Pontius Pilate in **"the morning"**[240](the Morning watch is 3:00 am – 6:00 am), and immediately after that statement tells of the fate of Judas in verses 3-10. Judas DIES of a HEAD WOUND in the MORNING.

Does any of this sound familiar? Granted, in this story Judas Iscariot is not killed by Jesus Christ, but is it not incredible how the watches in this story prophetically line up with the prophetic watches of the Time of the End, down to the Son of Perdition dying in the MORNING, just as the Antichrist will die at the MORNING of the 2nd Advent (6:00 am)?!

Now consider this: in **Revelation 2-3** there are 7 letters to 7 churches that contain hidden historical information relating to the Church Age as well as spiritual advice that anyone in any dispensation can benefit from. However, the direct teachings contained in these letters contradict the Pauline epistles[241], therefore the DOCTRINAL application must belong to End Time Jews, and it is arguable that each letter speaks of different kinds of disciples during those End Times. Take the letter to the church at Philadelphia in **Revelation 3:7-13** for example. These verses contain so much astounding information pertaining to the "Philadelphian Church period" (AD 1500-1900) that it is easy to completely overlook the doctrinal aspect of the passage:
Revelation 3:8 I know thy works: behold, I have set before thee an <u>OPEN DOOR</u> (Hello Matthew 25 and Song of Solomon 5!) and no man can shut it: for thou hast a little strength...
Their spirit was willing, and yes, their flesh was weak, but at least these particular Jews had a LITTLE strength.

---

[240] Matthew 27:1 When the <u>morning</u> was come, all the chief priests and elders of the people took counsel against Jesus to put him to death:
v.2 And when they had bound him, they led *him* away, and delivered him to Pontius Pilate the governor.
[241] Revelation 2:10 ...ye shall have TRIBULATION ten days...
v.11 ...he that OVERCOMETH shall not be hurt of the second death....
v.13 ...I know....where thou dwellest, even where SATAN'S seat is....
v.26 ...he that OVERCOMETH, and keepeth my works unto THE END....
3:4 ...he that OVERCOMETH, the same shall be clothed in white rainment....
v.12 Him that OVERCOMETH will I make a pillar in the temple of my God....
v.21 To him that OVERCOMETH will I grant to sit with me in my throne....
106

...and hast (1) **kept my word, and** (2) **hast not denied my name.**

Peter, James and John blew it in this area: they did NOT
(1) keep (i.e. obey) the Lord's word of **"watch and pray"** and (2)
Peter denied his name.[242]

What is the reward for keeping his word and not denying his
name?

v.10 Because thou hast kept the word of my patience, <u>I also</u>
<u>will keep thee from the HOUR OF TEMPTATION</u>, which
shall come upon all the world, to try them that dwell upon the
earth.

Ohhhhhh, they will be kept from the HOUR when Judas Iscariot /
THE SON OF PERDITION / the Antichrist comes!!

Ohhhhhh, so then the **"HOUR OF TEMPTATION"** is another
name for THE **"GREAT TRIBULATION"** PERIOD (3 ½ years).
Hour of Temptation = Great Tribulation period.

Ohhhhhh, so the Jews' <u>passing into</u> the hour of temptation or
<u>deliverance from</u> the hour of temptation is CONDITIONAL based
upon their ability to keep a COMMAND of Jesus!!

Ohhhhhh, and their deliverance FROM the **"hour of**
temptation" has something to do with a DOOR in HEAVEN (**v.7-**
8)!!

My, my; how the pieces of the puzzle begin to fit once a few of
the wrong pieces are removed or re-arranged.

To summarize, the rapture of the Church will occur sometime in
the very near future; at that moment ALL born again Christians
(dead and alive) will go up to Heaven and be MARRIED to Jesus
Christ. That event ushers in a 'transitional period' (if you will) to a
new 'End Time dispensation' (if you will again) that will last for **<u>a</u>**
<u>total of 10 ½ years</u>. The first 7 years are classified by Jesus as
"the beginning of sorrows" and the final 3 ½ years as a time of
"great tribulation". Sometime between the rapture of the Church
and Satan's Advent there will be a CONDITIONAL rapture of

---

[242] **Matthew 26:73 And after a while came unto** *him* **they that stood by, and said to**
Peter, Surely thou also art *one* **of them; for thy speech bewrayeth thee.**
v.74 Then began he to curse and to swear, *saying,* **<u>I know not the man.</u>**

Jewish saints that is based upon whether they are watching and praying or NOT. This rapture is obviously related to an End Time person's profession of faith, but is not <u>guaranteed</u> by that profession of faith. Also, seeing as how this is a rapture that is conditional upon watchfulness, it is obvious that a person has to be ALIVE to fulfill the condition: that is, this rapture is ONLY for those saints who are ALIVE and the rapture toward the end of the Great Tribulation is only for those saints who are DEAD.

CHAPTER 13

Future Doctrine to the 7 Churches

It would be beneficial here to explain how all of this information correlates with the 7 letters to the 7 churches and demonstrate how it all ties in perfectly with the content therein. An entire book could be written on Revelation chapters 2 and 3 alone, but rather than examine every detail of every verse, I will simply give an overview and comment on the salient points as they occur.

It must not be forgotten that all Scripture has three primary applications: Historical, Practical (or Spiritual) and Doctrinal. That is to say, all Scripture is connected to HISTORY whether directly or indirectly, by recording the events and teachings of the past, present and future. All Scripture has a PRACTICAL (or Spiritual) application in that there are lessons that can be learned and applied to our lives throughout. All Scripture has a DOCTRINAL application in that its teaching applies directly to someone at sometime and must be heeded by that person at that time. This of course is the area where **"rightly dividing the word of truth"**[243] is of utmost importance because even though **"all scripture is profitable for doctrine"**[244], not all of the doctrine in Scripture directly applies to all people at all times. An obvious example of this is Noah vs the New Testament Christian. God's **"doctrine"** (teaching) for Noah was to build an ark to save his family from a coming flood; this is NOT God's doctrine for ANY Christian in the Church Age. **Genesis 6:14**[245] is indeed DOCTRINE, but it is simply not doctrine FOR us today.

In the same way, the 7 letters to the 7 churches have historical, practical and doctrinal significance. At the time John wrote the book of Revelation (AD 95), the HISTORICAL application was primarily future (prophetic). It is unlikely that after the vision, John sent 7 different letters in the mail to 7 different literal churches

---

[243] 2 Timothy 2:15
[244] 2 Timothy 3:16
[245] Genesis 6:14 Make thee an ark of gopher wood; rooms shalt thou make in the ark, and shalt pitch it within and without with pitch.

109

across Asia Minor. He MAY have, but some of those letters would have presented a great deal of doctrinal confusion to some of those Christians living at that time. Just when those Smyrnian Christians thought they had a handle on Pauline doctrine and eternal security, here comes a letter from the Apostle John saying that if they are faithful unto death, God will give them a crown of life, and the reward for overcoming will be that they will not be hurt of the second death[246]?! WHAT?! Incredible mental gymnastics are required to explain these letters in a literal historical, Church Age context; therefore the historical aspect of these 7 letters fits much better over in the End Times OR as prophetic historical content that outlines the general condition of the Church over the last 1,984 years[247]. The latter provides us with a truly awesome insight to the omniscience of God: if Revelation chapters 2 and 3 indeed summarize and cover the time period of history extending from the Acts of the Apostles to the rapture of the Church, then that means that the Bible covers and comments on ALL OF HISTORY, from when TIME BEGAN to when TIME ENDS!!! The Bible is the only book on the planet like this. It gives us the story of the creation of the universe, tells us about history's first man and woman, and takes us up to the time of the global flood. Even though over 1,500 years elapse from Adam to Noah, the Bible still gives us the exact chronology of that time in Genesis 5. Then we have a historical record extending from Noah's exit from the ark all the way up to the rebuilding of Jerusalem by Nehemiah. The word of God then goes silent for nearly 400 years, and on the surface appears to have a missing time gap in what up to this point has been a perfect historical record, but if you go back a few books and re-read Daniel chapter 11, you find an incredible account of future history extending from the kingdom of Persia to the broken Grecian kingdom of Alexander to the time of the Maccabees, just prior to Christ's arrival. Matthew and Luke then record the birth of

---

[246] **Revelation 2:10 Fear none of those things which thou shalt suffer: behold, the devil shall cast *some* of you into prison, that ye may be tried; and ye shall have tribulation ten days: <u>be thou faithful unto death, and I will give thee a crown of life.</u> v.11 He that hath an ear, let him hear what the Spirit saith unto the churches; <u>He that overcometh shall not be hurt of the second death.</u>**
[247] Counting from AD 33 to AD 2017.

110

Jesus Christ and Luke continues the record all the way up to Paul's imprisonment in Rome.

The rest of the Bible is mostly epistles and doctrinal subject matter. The Book of Revelation contains future history that has not yet occurred as of the year 2017[248], but then the question arises, where is the Biblical historical narrative of last 2,000 years? Is it missing? Amazingly, when Revelation chapters 2-3 are examined in the light of history, we find that the spiritual condition of the 7 churches chronologically matches the general condition of the Body of Christ over the last 2 millennia! The **Ephesus** church was adamant about truth and heresy especially as it related to the APOSTLES, which is the outstanding characteristic of believers during the first couple hundred years after Calvary. The **Smyrna** church experienced horrendous persecution just as believers did from the time of the apostles to the time of Constantine. The **Pergamos** church was accused of mixing with the heathen, learning their ways, and getting messed up in doctrine, which is exactly what we find going on during the formative years of the official Roman Catholic Church (Constantine to Pope Gregory). The letter to the **Thyatira** church is full of scathing judgment against the Jezebel who is seducing God's servants to join her idolatrous religion. This time period is known, even by secular historians, as the DARK AGES and Bible Believers had such difficulty just trying to survive that the Lord simply told them to hold fast what they had and that He would put upon them "none other burden". The **Sardis** church has a reputation of life and orthodox Christianity, but is said to be DEAD. As the Roman Catholic church entered into the height of its global power, true Bible Believing Christianity continued to be stamped out and remain underground. It was not until the Lord brought the word of God back out into the open through men like Martin Luther and William Tyndale that light began to once again shine upon mankind. Just as Jesus Christ's resurrection brought light and life to a darkened world, so the resurrection of the Scriptures from the tomb of Roman Catholic monasteries brought life and light to a darkened world. During this **Philadelphia** church period, history

---

[248] The year this thesis was written.

records the spiritual breakthroughs of the Protestant Reformation (Europe) and Great Awakening (America). Now that Satan had lost his grip on the Scriptures and they were out in the open, he had to resort to his *modus operandi* and once convince God's people to doubt, disobey and CORRUPT the word of God[249]. Around the turn of the 20th century, the world was introduced to the RV (England) and the ASV (America) which opened the flood gates to over 200 new Bible versions that plunged the church into its final state of total apostasy depicted by the **Laodicea** church.

The approximate dates that these 7 churches correspond to are as follows:

1. Ephesus   33 - 100
2. Smyrna   100 - 325
3. Pergamos   325 - 500
4. Thatira   500 - 1,000
5. Sardis   1,000 - 1,500
6. Philadelphia   1,500 - 1,900
7. Laodicea   1,900 - Church rapture

Revelation 2-3 gives the complete historical summary of the Church Age and goes on to record the events of the Time of the End and the 1,000 year reign of Jesus Christ that follows. Revelation 20 is the final end of time as we know it, and Revelation 21 is Creation 2.0. Every moment of human history, from beginning to end was pre-recorded in the Scriptures IF you concede that the 7 letters to the 7 churches represent the Church Age, which of course, they do.

The next application of Revelation 2-3 is PRACTICAL; that is, anyone at anytime can gain useful instruction from the content of these letters. For example, the letter to Ephesus is a good reminder not to become so consumed with serving the Lord that we get away from our relationship with Him. The Philadelphia church is the only church that is given zero reproof and just happens to be the

---

[249] Genesis 3:1 ...Yea, hath God said...?

only church that is said to have kept God's word[250], the lesson being, if we want to be fruitful, we must be diligent to heed and hold on to the Scriptures. The Laodicean church shows us what the Lord sees in a Christian who is too attached to worldly riches. Suffice it to say, there is plenty of practical lessons to be learned from these letters.

The most important aspect of the Scripture is the third aspect, which is its DOCTRINAL application. There is no subjectivity here, and Bible Believers must determine WHO this material is directed toward. The natural assumption is that these chapters apply doctrinally to Christians in the Church Age because they are written to **"churches"**; we are going to have to think a little bit harder than that though. A "church" is simply an assembly of believers; therefore A "church" is not always a reference to THE "Church" (Body of Christ)[251] and a "church" is not something that is limited to the CHURCH AGE. There can and will be assemblies of believers in the Time of the End after the Body of Christ has been raptured, and even though they are not part of THE Church (universal organism) they can still be part of A church (local organization). This means that the 7 letters can indeed be DOCTRINALLY applicable to someone other than Church Age Christians, which is exactly what we discover them to be.

You will quickly notice that much of the instruction given in these two chapters cannot possibly be applied literally and doctrinally to Christians in the Church Age. The word "overcome" appears no less than seven times in these two chapters, but by simply linking it to a Christian in the sense that he "overcomes" the world through faith in Christ[252] eliminates the meaning of the Lord's message entirely. The Lord is giving each church some INSTRUCTION which IF they will heed, they will be REWARDED. What would be the point in a WARNING about

---

[250] **Revelation 3:10 Because thou hast <u>kept the word of my patience</u>, I also will keep thee from the hour of temptation, which shall come upon all the world, to try them that dwell upon the earth.**
[251] **Acts 7:38 This is he, that was in <u>the church</u> in the wilderness** (Old Testament Jews coming out of Egypt) **with the angel which spake to him in the mount Sina, and** *with* **our fathers: who received the lively oracles to give unto us:**
[252] **1 John 5:5 Who is he that overcometh the world, but he that believeth that Jesus is the Son of God?**

failure and the INCENTIVE of a reward if "overcoming" was automatically included with salvation?! Obviously, there is a possibility that the ones that these letters are written to will be capable of either failing or overcoming, and those who fail will be punished and those who overcome will be rewarded. In one instance, the reward for obedience is getting to eat of **"the tree of life"**[253] and in another instance the punishment for failing is being **"hurt of the second death"**[254]! Does that sound anything like Church Age Christianity? Absolutely NOT; so we have to look beyond a self-centered approach of *"God wrote everything in the entire Bible for ME"* and determine who this portion of Scripture is written to doctrinally.

 I contend that these 7 letters are doctrinally applicable to believers in the Time of the End, and likely describe 7 different 'types' or 'groups' of people whereby any End Time believer could identify with. The basic premise of each message is the same, namely that they need to be obedient and overcome, and beware of failing lest they suffer a grievous punishment. This links all 7 churches together under a common 'dispensation' (the End Times), and I am not at all suggesting that there are 7 different plans of salvation in the last days. They all have the same common denominator but vary on the details, and as will be seen, there is a very logical reason for this.

 Let us now consider the doctrinal highlights of these 7 churches, and how they relate to believers in the Time of the End:

Ephesus: Revelation 2:1-7
 The warning is that they have left their first **"LOVE"**. The significance of this becomes disturbing when contemplated in the light of the Song of Solomon. The woman's great love for her Beloved has grown cold, and she is said to have **"fallen"** and needs to repent or else the Lord will come **"quickly"** and will remove their **"CANDLESTICK"**. This immediately brings to mind Jesus' parable of the wise and foolish virgins, which, as we

---

[253] **Revelation 2:7 ...To him that overcometh will I give to eat of the tree of life, which is in the midst of the paradise of God.**

[254] **Revelation 2:11 ...He that overcometh shall not be hurt of the second death.**

114

have seen, speaks of a conditional rapture. The foolish virgins slept and their lamps went out. When the Lord came at an hour they were not expecting him, they were unprepared like the woman in Song of Solomon who had **"put off [her] coat"**. The Ephesus church represents believing Jews who are alive toward the very beginning of the Time of the End. The Great Tribulation has not started yet, and the conditional rapture has not occurred yet. Their fate is still in their own hands, and if they overcome, be it by rapture or martyrdom, they will be granted access to the tree of life in Heaven[255]. Unless the fruit of that tree is just really tasty, the incentive of access to the tree of life is pointless to someone who is born again and already has eternal life. Verse 7 insinuates that the recipient of this reward does NOT HAVE eternal life, but will be rewarded with it if he overcomes; that is to say, faith AND WORKS are a requirement for salvation after Church is raptured out and the Time of the End begins, which makes perfect sense given the fact that in the End Times, God's servants are preaching the Gospel of the KINGDOM OF HEAVEN and not the Gospel of the Grace of God.

Smyrna: Revelation 2:8-11

This church represents a group of people that will suffer greatly at the hand of **"the DEVIL"** himself and will have **"tribulation ten days"**. This church represents the End Time believers who are servants of the Lord, but missed the conditional rapture. It is interesting that the word "Smyrna" means "myrrh" and the woman in Song of Solomon 5, who hesitated when her Beloved was at the door and subsequently could not find him, is said to have hands that **"dropped with myrrh"** and **"fingers with sweet smelling myrrh"**. The connection between this woman, the smell of myrrh, and the Smyrna believers having to go through ten years of tribulation is no coincidence. They have ten years of tribulation to endure, and if they remain faithful and overcome, they will be rewarded with a **"crown of life"** and **"shall not be hurt of the**

---

[255] **Revelation 2:7** says that the tree of life is **"in the midst of the paradise of God"**. There is no need to assume that this is in the heart of the earth as it was before Calvary, because we know from **2 Corinthians 12:4** that paradise is now UP IN HEAVEN.

second death".

Pergamos: Revelation 2:12-17

Satan and Satan's seat are mentioned here which means the doctrinal content of this letter can be applied to believers living during the final 3 ½ years of Great Tribulation, for at this time **"Satan [will be] cast out into the earth"**[256]. There is no admonition to 'watch' in this letter because the conditional rapture is long gone and the only hope of these believers is to overcome by enduring to the end. This Pergamos classification of believers will have problems related to EATING the king's dainty meat that has been sacrificed to a talking IDOL[257]! The Lord notices the man named Antipas who was MATRYRED among them; the observation of this man and the meaning of his name is by no means an accident, for his name means "against everything" which is precisely the demeanor that will be required of God's people who are alive during the Great Tribulation. The Lord tells this group that He is coming and will **"fight against them with the sword of [His] mouth"** and that they need to be sure and **"repent"**, lest they too fall with the wicked. If they will be faithful, God promises to FEED THEM HIMSELF with **"the hidden MANNA"**. This will be a precious promise to those Jews who will be **"in the wilderness"** for **"a time, and times, and half a time"** fleeing from the **"face of the serpent"**[258]. Those tribulation Jews will be **"nourished"** with **"manna"** just as their fathers were during the Exodus from Egypt. The theme of this entire letter is consistent with the circumstances of the Great Tribulation and 2nd Advent.

---

[256] Revelation 12:9 And the great dragon was cast out, that old serpent, called the Devil, and Satan, which deceiveth the whole world: he was cast out into the earth, and his angels were cast out with him.
[257] Revelation 13:15 And he had power to give life unto the <u>image of the beast</u>, that the image of the beast should both <u>speak</u>, and cause that as many as would not worship the image of the beast should be killed.
[258] Revelation 12:14 And to the woman were given two wings of a great eagle, that she might fly into <u>the wilderness</u>, into her place, where she is <u>nourished</u> for <u>a time, and times, and half a time</u>, from <u>the face of the serpent.</u>

116

Thyatira: Revelation 2:18-29

This church represents a group of believers who are around before and after Satan's Advent. They have issues with **"Jezebel"** and her idolatrous religion, which is directly tied to Mystery Babylon and the Roman Catholic Church. This whorish religion will be in vogue from the start of the End Time until shortly after Satan's Advent, at which time he will have her burned with fire[259]. The Lord said that he would give this wicked woman **"space to repent of her fornication"** but since she will not repent, he will **"cast her…and them that commit adultery with her into great tribulation"**. This implies that the Thyatira class of believers are around BEFORE and DURING the Great Tribulation. Once again, there is no admonition to "watch" and no rebuke for not watching, so this church is likely representative of a believer who had no knowledge of a conditional rapture or became a believer after that rapture took place. For **"keeping [the Lord's] works unto the end"** this believer will be rewarded with **"the MORNING star"** (Jesus Christ), which again is another allusion to the NIGHT of the End Time and the 2nd Advent occurring during the MORNING WATCH.

Sardis: Revelation 3:1-6

Now we are presented with a church that identifies a group of believers who are connected to the conditional rapture. They are given warning to 'get right' in verses 1-3 and told that if they do not **"WATCH"**, the Lord would come upon them as a **"THIEF"**. The Lord alludes to this concept of the thief a number of times, and the application can be confusing and contradictory if isolated to a single event. Jesus said in **John 10:10, "The thief cometh not, but for to steal, and to kill, and to destroy: I am come that they might have life, and that they might have *it* more abundantly"**. Jesus CONTRASTS Himself with the thief while He is trying to win the Jewish people, but the Jews rejected Him and **"numbered [Him] with the transgressors"**[260] while the Romans hung him up

---

[259] Revelation 17:16 And the ten horns which thou sawest upon the beast, these shall hate the whore, and shall make her desolate and naked, and shall eat her flesh, and burn her with fire.
[260] Isaiah 53:12

between two thieves. Evidently, the Lord's attitude towards this is, if they are going to TREAT Him like a thief, then He is going to ACT like a thief, and do the three things that Jesus said a thief would do: 1) Steal 2) Kill 3) Destroy ...and in that order:

1) TO STEAL

Matthew, Mark and Luke each record Jesus making a statement along the lines of watching and being ready for someone's sudden coming. Interestingly enough, all three of them recognize the unexpected visitor as THE LORD. Matthew calls **Him "your Lord"**[261], Luke calls Him **"the lord"**[262], and Mark calls Him **"the master"**[263] and Matthew and Luke's statements are in the context of **"the THIEF"**! The Lord Himself is the THIEF who STEALS from the HOUSE of Israel, except He does not take OBJECTS, He takes PEOPLE! **Matthew 24:42-47, Mark 13:32-37, and Luke 12:35-40** are all passages that speak of this conditional rapture, and the recurring theme is a wedding, a feast, a watch in the night, and a thief.

This conditional rapture application of the **"thief"** is also found in **Revelation 16:15 Behold, I come as a <u>thief</u>. Blessed *is* he that <u>watcheth</u>, and <u>keepeth his garments</u>, <u>lest he walk naked</u>, and they see his <u>shame</u>.**

The Jews are to **"watch"** for the **"thief"**, and in so doing, they will **"[keep] their garments"** and not **"walk** (spiritually) **naked"** and be **"[ashamed]"** at the Lord's 2nd Advent. Notice that this is exactly what he told the SARDIS church: **"If therefore thou shalt not WATCH, I will come on thee as a THIEF...Thou hast a few names even in Sardis which have not defiled their GARMENTS: and they shall WALK with me in WHITE: for they are worthy. He that overcometh, the same shall be clothed in WHITE RAIMENT..."**

---

[261] **Matthew 24:42 Watch therefore: for ye know not what hour <u>your Lord</u> doth come.**

[262] **Luke 12:37 Blessed *are* those servants, whom <u>the lord</u> when he cometh shall find watching: verily I say unto you, that he shall gird himself, and make them to sit down to meat, and will come forth and serve them.**

[263] **Mark 13:35 Watch ye therefore: for ye know not when <u>the master</u> of the house cometh, at even, or at midnight, or at the cockcrowing, or in the morning:**

118

The first installment of **"the thief"** is the conditional rapture of Jewish saints that takes place during the time of the Beginning of Sorrows.

2) TO KILL

The second installment of **"the thief"** involves killing which begins with the Great Tribulation and continues up to the 2nd Advent,

1 Thessalonians 5:2 For yourselves know perfectly that <u>the day of the Lord</u> so cometh as a <u>thief</u> in the night.
v.3 For when they shall say, Peace and safety; then sudden destruction cometh upon them, as travail upon a woman with child; and they shall not escape.
v.4 But ye, brethren, are not in darkness, that <u>that day</u> should overtake you as a <u>thief</u>.

The **"day of the Lord"** in this particular passage is not the 2nd Advent, it is the start of the Great Tribulation. The unregenerate world will not be saying **"peace and safety"** after 3 ½ years of Satan ruling the earth and the worst catastrophes the world has ever seen! Also, the **"peace and safety"** is not during the *"first 3 ½ years of the Tribulation period"* because <u>there is no first 3 ½ years of the Tribulation period!</u> Besides, the time preceding the Great Tribulation is called **"the beginning of SORROWS"** (not **"peace and safety"**) and furthermore, the Red Horseman brings in a World War during that time, NOT **"peace and safety"**. The Bible tells you EXACTLY when the world says **"peace and safety"**:

Revelation 13:3 And I saw one of his heads as it were wounded to death; and his deadly wound was healed: and <u>all the world</u> wondered after the beast.
v.4 And they <u>worshipped</u> the dragon which gave power unto the beast: and they <u>worshipped</u> the beast, saying, Who *is* like unto the beast? <u>who is able to make war with him?</u>

When the Antichrist rises from the dead (Satan's Advent), the entire world marvels at this and all declare **"who is able to make war with him?"**; in other words, *"who could kill a man who has conquered death"*? The answer is, NO ONE, and so the next question is *"who could make war against a man who has* *conquered death?"* and the answer again is NO ONE. At THIS moment in history, the warring in the world stops. This resurrection from the dead grabs the attention of the entire earth and people stop WARRING and start WONDERING. At this time, the world declares **"peace and safety"** under the rule of their savior, THE ANTICHRIST, but as the Scripture says, **"then SUDDEN destruction cometh upon them"**. The 3 ½ year Great Tribulation officially begins and the Lord wastes no time telling those 7 angels to blow those 7 trumpets; **"and they** (the world) **shall not escape"**. The thief KILLS over half of the entire earth's population through global plagues and KILLS so many soldiers at the Battle of Armageddon that the **"blood came out...even unto the horse bridles, by the space of a thousand and six hundred furlongs"**[264].

3) TO DESTROY

The third installment of **"the thief"** involves the destruction of the creation at the end of the Millennium:

2 Peter 3:10 But the day of the Lord will come as a <u>thief</u> in the night; in the which <u>the heavens shall pass away</u> with a great noise, and <u>the elements shall melt with fervent heat</u>, the earth also and the works that are therein shall be <u>burned up</u>.
v.11 *Seeing* then *that* all these things shall be <u>dissolved</u>, what manner *of persons* ought ye to be in *all* holy conversation and godliness,
v.12 Looking for and hasting unto the coming of the day of God, wherein <u>the heavens being on fire shall be dissolved</u>, and <u>the elements shall melt with fervent heat</u>?
v.13 Nevertheless we, according to his promise, look for <u>new heavens and a new earth</u>, wherein dwelleth righteousness.

It could be argued that verse 10 is talking about the Battle of Armageddon (start of the Millennium) as opposed to the Battle of Gog and Magog (end of the Millennium), however the rest of the context is unmistakably referring to Revelation 20, 21 and 22 which describes the destruction of the universe and subsequent creation of the new heavens and new earth. Furthermore, Peter

---

[264] **Revelation 14:20**
120

conveniently reminds the reader just two verses PRIOR to this passage that **"one day** (the day of the Lord) **is with the Lord as a thousand years, and a thousand years as one day"**! The connection is to the END of the Millennium, and notice once again that the Lord likens this DESTRUCTION to the work of **"a THIEF"**!!

John 10:10 The THIEF cometh not, but for to STEAL (conditional rapture during the Beginning of Sorrows)**, and to KILL** (Great Tribulation to the Battle of Armageddon at the 2nd Advent / START of the Millennium)**, and to DESTROY** (Battle of Gog and Magog at the END of the Millennium)**: I am come** (during the Church Age) **that they might have life, and that they might have *it* more abundantly.**

Philadelphia: Revelation 3:7-13

This church represents End Time believers who are obedient in all things and will therefore receive the greatest reward: <u>escape from the coming Great Tribulation period!</u> Notice that the Lord begins this letter with talk about an **"open DOOR"** that only He has the **"key"** to, and only He can open and shut.

Hmmm, I wonder: what <u>door</u> could He possibly be talking about?

Because this Philadelphia class of believers **"kept the word of [the Lord's] patience"**, the Lord promises to **"keep [them] from the hour of temptation, which shall come upon all the world, to try them that dwell upon the earth"**. As noted in a previous chapter, the **"hour of temptation"** involves the appearance of the Son of Perdition and is directly connected with the start of the Great Tribulation period. The Lord is promising these End Time believers that He will keep them from the Great Tribulation, and the way that He will do that is by means of an OPEN DOOR in HEAVEN! <u>This church represents those believers who will be raptured out of the world during the time of the Beginning of Sorrows.</u>

This passage is can be used as a proof text for a number of truths, such as the supremacy of the King James Bible, the pre-tribulation rapture of the Church, and now the conditional rapture of End Times saints. It is important however that Bible teachers draw clear lines between these applications. The first is a HISTORICAL application, the second is a SPIRITUAL application, and the third is a DOCTRINAL application. This verse CANNOT be doctrinally to Church Age Christians because the obvious question arises, *"what if a Christian does NOT keep 'the word of his patience'?"* to which the underline answer is, *"he would miss the Church rapture and go though the Tribulation period"*. Once again, this demonstrates the folly of attempting to doctrinally apply End Time Scripture to Church Age believers, which results in astute people seeing the glaring discrepancy and then ignorantly concluding that pre-Tribulation rapture theology is a contrived lie, that the Church has replaced Israel and is destined to suffer the "pre-wrath" or "post-wrath" of the Great Tribulation period. The passage certainly speaks of a rapture, it just does not speak of the Church's rapture.

The Lord reiterates His caution by telling End Time, Philadelphia class of believers, **"Behold, I come quickly"**, and as we have seen from other passages, the implied admonition is to **"WATCH"** and be ready for His sudden coming during the time of the Beginning of Sorrows:

Mark 13:35 Watch ye therefore: for ye know not when the master of the house cometh…
v.36 Lest coming suddenly he find you sleeping.
v.37 And what I say unto you I say unto all, Watch.

Laodicea: Revelation 3:14-22

Finally, this church represents the 7th class of believers during the Time of the End, the class of believers who are so consumed with earthly riches that they run the risk of missing the conditional rapture and are setting themselves up for failure when the mark of the Beast becomes available. These End Time believers are the type who want Jesus, but want the world also. They evidently know not that **"the friendship of the world is enmity with God"**[265] and so Jesus counsels them to release their wealth (**"buy"**) in exchange for suffering (**"gold tried in the fire"**). This is absolutely foolish to the world's wisdom, but if obeyed will result in REWARD (**"that thou mayest be rich"**) and

---

[265] James 4:4

122

CLOTHING (**"and white raiment that thou mayest be clothed, and that the shame of thy nakedness do not appear"**) and SIGHT (**"and anoint thine eyes with eyesalve, that thou mayest see"**). These three elements of reward, clothing and sight[266] are all affiliated with the conditional rapture.

The Lord then says, **"As many as I love, I rebuke and chasten"**. Failure to obey will result in a rebuke and chastening from the Lord, and one possible application is that the 'rebuke' involves missing the conditional rapture and being left behind during the time of the Beginning of Sorrows and the 'chastening' has to do with going through the Great Tribulation.

Jesus concludes His final letter with the statement, **"Behold, I stand at the door, and knock: if any man hear my voice, and open the door, I will come in to him, and will sup with him, and he with me.**

Once again, there are multiple practical applications that could be made from this verse ranging from Jesus knocking on the door of a sinner's heart to the Lord standing outside of a church building desiring to be a part of the service, but his knock cannot be heard over the decibels of the rock concert going on inside. The DOCTRINAL application however is clearly aimed at an End Time believer who has an opportunity to escape the coming Great Tribulation period. The DOOR, the KNOCKING, the VOICE, the SUPPER[267]: the components of the conditional rapture are all there.

Any Bible Believer must concede that the warnings and commands in these 7 letters must be LITERAL for someone at sometime, and although anyone with a dispensational understanding of the Scriptures can clearly see that these letters apply doctrinally to End Time believers, to date there is no popularly accepted eschatological theory that can provide an answer as to WHAT all of the statements contained therein mean.

---

[266] The **"eyesalve"** is more than likely TEARS of REPENTANCE. This speaks of HUMBLENESS which is absolutely critical in the End Times. If Jews do not weep early on in the Time of the End, they will weep later on when they will be **"rejected"** and find **"no place of repentance"** though they seek it **"carefully with tears". Hebrews 12:17**
[267] As in a MARRIAGE SUPPER!

Interpreting Revelation 2-3 in light of a <u>10 Year long</u> Time of the End that includes a <u>conditional rapture</u> allows for a <u>doctrinal explanation</u> of all things contained in the 7 letters that is <u>consistent</u> with other <u>Kingdom of Heaven</u> passages of Scripture. 7 year and 4 year tribulation theology leave no allowance for an additional, conditional rapture, and consequently have no DOCTRINAL solution for the cryptic statements contained in these 7 letters and can only offer spiritualized applications that are ambiguous at best.

CHAPTER 14

The Timeline Chart

This chapter is dedicated to the progressive charts that illustrate the theories discussed in this thesis.

Chart 5 shows the entire Time of the End beginning with the rapture of the Church and ending with the 2nd Advent of Jesus Christ. The rapture of the Church happens in the <u>EVENING</u> (6 pm) at the end of daytime just before the NIGHT begins (the night being a type of the entire End Time period). The night ends when the SON / SUN arises in the <u>MORNING</u> (6 am).

The entire Time of the End (NIGHT) is divided into 4 watches:
1. Evening   6:00 pm –   9:00 pm
2. Midnight   9:00 pm – 12:00 am
3. Cockcrowing   12:00 am –   3:00 am
4. Morning   3:00 am –   6:00 am

CHART 5

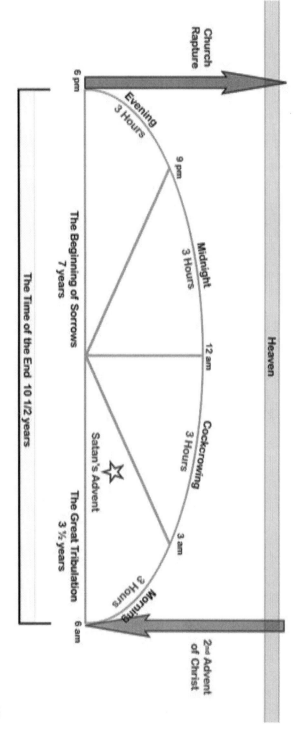

Heaven

Church Rapture

2ⁿᵈ Advent of Christ

6 pm

Evening
3 Hours

9 pm

Midnight
3 Hours

12 am

Cockcrowing
3 Hours

3 am

Satan's Advent

Morning
3 Hours

6 am

The Beginning of Sorrows
7 years

The Great Tribulation
3 ½ years

The Time of the End 10 1/2 years

There are exactly **10 ½ years from the rapture of the Church to the 2nd Advent**. The rapture of the Church occurs in the spring season (around Passover) and the 2nd advent occurs 10 years later in the fall season (around the Feast of Tabernacles).

Here is the mathematical breakdown between the prophetic hours of the night and the 10 ½ literal years of the Time of the End:

10 ½ years = 12 hours of the night

12 hours / 10 ½ years = 1.14 prophetic hours per literal year

To determine exactly where the 3 ½ year Great Tribulation fits on this graph, we have to first multiply 3 ½ years by 1.14 hrs/yr which equals 3.99 hours. Therefore, 3 ½ years is equal to approximately 4 hours of the night. The Great Tribulation ends with the 2nd Advent, so the final 4 hours of the night are 3 ½ years of Great Tribulation, placed at the end of chart 6:

CHART 6

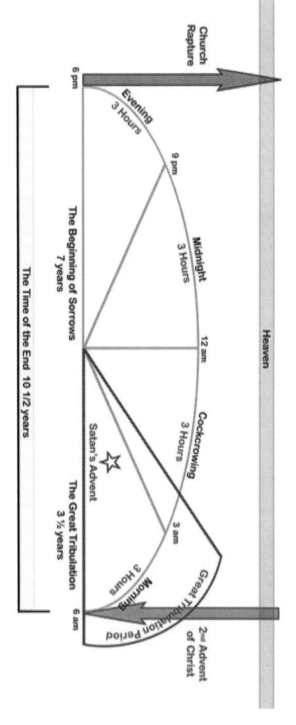

Church
Rapture

Heaven

Evening
3 Hours

9 pm

Midnight
3 Hours

12 am

Cockcrowing
3 Hours

3 am

Satan's Advent

☆

3 Hours
Morning

Great Tribulation Period

6 am

2nd Advent
of Christ

6 pm

The Beginining of Sorrows
7 years

The Great Tribulation
3½ years

The Time of the End 10 1/2 years

128

Notice that the Antichrist's resurrection (Satan's Advent – **Matthew 24:15**) occurs during the Cockcrowing Watch, and if this chart had all 12 hours of the night written out, the Antichrist would come slightly after 2:00 am.

As an interesting side note, Jesus Christ told Simon Peter (who, by the way, was the Apostle to the Jews / Israel) **"Verily I say unto thee, That this day, even this night, before the cock crow TWICE, thou shalt deny me THRICE."**[268] That very night the Son of Perdition shows up (Judas Iscariot) and shortly thereafter, Peter denies the Lord 3 times. The connection of these elements, Peter's 3 denials, Judas Iscariot, and the cock crowing, is peculiar. Prophetically, these three things will occur again: Satan incarnate (type: Judas Iscariot) comes around the Cockcrowing watch of the prophetic "night of the End Times", and by the time of Satan's Advent, the Jews as a nation have denied / rejected Jesus Christ 3 times:

1. During Jesus' Earthly Ministry   (ca-CAW!)
2. The Stoning of Stephen   (ca-CAW!)
3. The Rejection of the 144,000   (ca-CAW!)

Chart 7 shows the approximate occurrences of the 7 Seal Judgments, 7 Trumpet Judgments and 7 Vial Judgments.

The Man of Sin is the 1st seal, and the 4th seal is his resurrection from the dead, officially ushering in the final 3 ½ years of Great Tribulation (the last half of Daniel's 70th week). The first half of Daniel's 70th week is nowhere on this chart because it occurred back in AD 30-33. All of the trumpet and vial judgments occur AFTER the antichrist rises from the dead. The final 3 ½ years is also the time of the mark of the Beast. Seal judgments #2 and #3 occur BEFORE the final 3 ½ years, during the **"beginning of sorrows"**, but their exact location on this chart is subjective. Seal judgment #7 is the 2nd Advent, so obviously #5 and #6 happen between the start and end of the final 3 ½ years.

---

[268] **Mark 14:30**

CHART 7

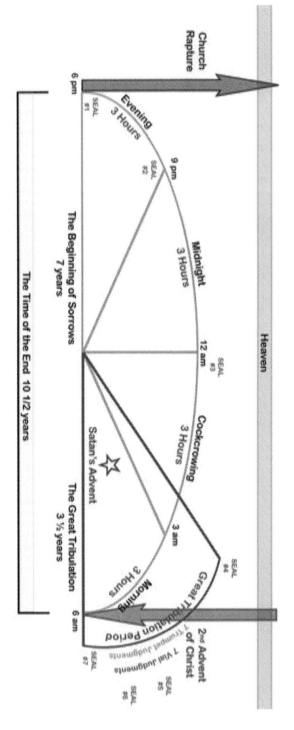

As for the conditional rapture of Jewish End Time saints, Jesus said that it would occur at MIDNIGHT[269]. This does not mean that it has to occur at 12 am on the dot; it could occur ANY TIME between 9 pm and 12 am and still have occurred at **"midnight"** because it would have occurred during the MIDNIGHT WATCH. This fits perfectly with the fact that the conditional rapture has to be WATCHED for, because no one knows the day or the hour wherein the Son of Man cometh. They may know that the THIEF is coming sometime during the midnight watch, but 3 prophetic hours in a watch is the equivalent of 3.42 years (1.14 hrs/yr x 3 hours = 3.42 years)!

As Chart 8 shows, Jesus Christ will **"stand at the door and knock"** sometime during that Midnight watch time frame. During this time it is CRITICAL for the Jews to WATCH for Jesus Christ. If they are paying attention, they will hear the **"knock"** and be raptured out through the DOOR in the sky and get in on the marriage feast up in heaven and skip out on the Great Tribulation.

---

[269] **Matthew 25:6 And at <u>midnight</u> there was a cry made, Behold, the bridegroom cometh; go ye out to meet him.**

CHART 8

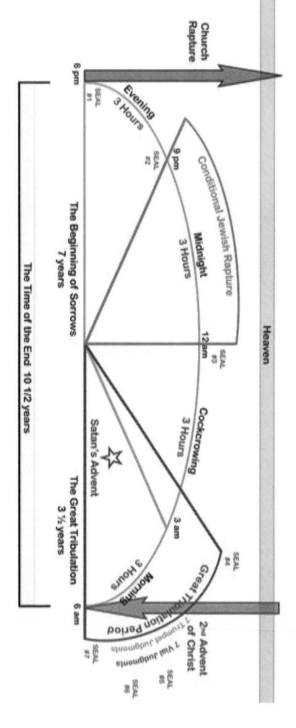

The Judgment Seat of Christ is for the CHURCH (Chart 9). The Marriage Supper of the Lamb takes place in Heaven and is primarily for the Church, but there will be some believing, watchful Jews on the earth that will have the opportunity to get in on it too. If a Jewish man is WATCHING and doing right, he will be prepared for the coming of the THEIF and will be TAKEN away to heaven, and the Lord will give that faithful steward his MEAT (marriage supper feast) in due season. The foolish Jews who knew their Lord's will, but did not watch, now have to ENDURE TO THE END to be saved. They either have to endure to the end of their LIFE and suffer a martyr's death, or endure to the end of the Great Tribulation and be physically rescued by Jesus Christ at the 2nd Advent. This salvation will be bitter-sweet in that they will be glad to be saved, but ashamed of themselves for not watching. All of the Jews who DO watch and get raptured will be clothed in white garments. The Jews who DO NOT watch will be left behind and will not receive any white garments and, in that sense, will be NAKED (spiritually) when Jesus returns. At the time of the 2nd Advent it will be abundantly obvious which Jews obeyed the Lord and which Jews did not. Those who did not obey will walk **"naked"**, that is, without the Lord's white robes, and everyone will see their shame. The nakedness is certainly spiritual, but could be physical too.

Revelation 16:15 Behold, I come as a thief. Blessed *is* he that WATCHETH, and keepeth his garments, lest (condition!) **he walk NAKED, and they** (those Jews who did obey) **see his shame** (at the 2nd Advent)**.**

Also remember that the lazy woman in **Song of Solomon 5** said **"I have put off my coat; how shall I put it on?"**. Her failure to WATCH for her beloved and her MISSING His coming is directly tied to her being NAKED. Seeing as how righteousness is frequently typified as a garment in the Bible[270], the prophetic interpretation here is that this woman (the Jews in the End Time) is

---

[270] **Job 29:14 I put on <u>righteousness</u>, and it <u>clothed</u> me...**
Psalm 132:9 Let thy priests be <u>clothed</u> with <u>righteousness</u>...
Isaiah 61:10 I will greatly rejoice in the LORD, my soul shall be joyful in my God; for he hath <u>clothed</u> me with the <u>garments of salvation</u>, he hath <u>covered</u> me with the <u>robe of righteousness</u>...

without righteousness and is disobedient to her Lord much like the foolish virgins[271], the preoccupied invitees[272], and the sleeping disciples[273] were.

Even though the date of the conditional rapture is unknown, the Lord gave many clues as to the specific timing of that event. We know that it will occur sometime during the Midnight watch, but as can be seen in Chart 8, that rapture can occur anytime during a 3.42 year time period (or 1,231 days)! Interestingly enough, the book of Esther sheds a little more light on the timing of this conditional rapture:

Esther 1:1 Now it came to pass in the days of Ahasuerus, (this *is* Ahasuerus which reigned, from India even unto Ethiopia, *over* an hundred and seven and twenty provinces:)
v.2 *That* in those days, when the king Ahasuerus sat on the throne of his kingdom, which *was* in Shushan the palace,
v.3 In the THIRD YEAR of his reign, he made a feast unto all his princes and his servants; the power of Persia and Media, the nobles and princes of the provinces, *being* before him:
v.4 When he shewed the riches of his glorious kingdom and the honour of his excellent majesty many days, *EVEN* AN HUNDRED AND FOURSCORE DAYS.
It mentions the third year of his reign and180 days which gives us 3 ½ years. How CONVENIENT!!
v.5 <u>And when these days were expired</u>, the king made a FEAST....
This is a SECOND feast that follows on the heels of the FIRST feast in **v.3**. There is no indication that there is any length of time between the two feasts, so for all practical purposes, this seems to be one big, long feast, except the first part of it was for the princes, and the second part is for the people. This second feast (or second part of the feast) is the one to pay close attention to:
...unto all the people that were present in Shushan the palace, both unto great and small, SEVEN DAYS, in the court of the

---

[271] **Matthew 25:1-13**
[272] **Luke14:15-24**
[273] **Matthew 26:36-46**

134

garden of the king's palace;

The fact that this is a SEVEN day feast indicates that it is a MARRIAGE FEAST. There are three reasons why this is the case:

1. A clear parallel is given in the Bible with Samson's marriage feast, which also lasts seven days:

Judges 14:12 And Samson said unto them, I will now put forth a riddle unto you: if ye can certainly declare it me within the SEVEN DAYS of the FEAST, and find *it* out, then I will give you thirty sheets and thirty change of garments:

2. There are SIX <u>specifically</u> mentioned marriage feasts in the Bible:

1) **Genesis 29:21-22** Jacob and Leah
2) **Judges 14** Samson and the Philistine Woman
3) **Esther 2:18** Ahasuerus and Esther
4) **Matthew 22:1-14** The Parable of the King's Son
5) **John 2:1** The Wedding at Cana of Galilee
6) **Revelation 19:9** Jesus Christ and the Church

As just about anyone who reads their Bible knows, the Lord's favorite number is 7. There is NO WAY that He is going to leave these six feasts hanging in His book, and so without a DOUBT, the feast in **Esther 1** is a MARRIAGE FEAST celebrating the marriage of Ahasuerus and Vashti!

7) **Esther 1** Ahasuerus and Vashti
The fact that this is the only marriage feast in the Bible that is between two GENTILES may be why the Lord leaves the nature of this event somewhat concealed.

3. The feast in **Esther 2:18** that celebrates the King's marriage to Esther bears some striking similarities to the feast that we read about in chapter 1, which indicates that the feast in chapter 1 was indeed a celebration of the King's marriage to Vashti: both were made for the princes and the servants (**1:3, 2:18**), both had gifts that were given according to the state of the king (**1:7, 2:18**), and the wife wears the crown royal in both accounts (**1:11, 2:17**).

The peculiar thing to notice is that the text in chapter 1 records 3 ½ years and then 7 days. The 7 <u>days</u> of feasting for the people are a type of the 7 <u>years</u> of feasting for the Jews who will be raptured out during the Midnight watch. Granted, the passage does not say 7 YEARS, nevertheless, the connection between a '3 ½ ' and a '7' is certainly interesting, especially when the context is a MARRIAGE FEAST! So, similar to what we see in the book of Esther, there will be a '3 ½', and then a '7', except in the context of the End Times, there will be 3 ½ YEARS that transpire on the earth after the Church is raptured. Then a <u>Marriage Feast</u> will begin in Heaven which will last for <u>7 YEARS</u>. Added together, this equals 10 ½ years, which is the total length of the Time of the End. If this account in Esther is indeed a clue as to when the heavenly wedding feast will be accessible to **"the people"** (the Jews on the earth), <u>then it would indicate that the conditional rapture will not happen for at least 3 ½ years after the rapture of the Church.</u> As stated above, 3 ½ years is the equivalent of 4 hours of the night, and (lo and behold!) **<u>4 hours past the Church rapture (6 pm) puts you in the MIDNIGHT WATCH (10 pm)!</u>**

This is VERY interesting because this reveals that there are three major End Time events that will occur at ONE-THIRD intervals (3 ½ years) of the 10 ½ year long Time of the End.

Observe: the starting event is the rapture of the Church at the beginning of the Evening watch (6 pm). 3 ½ years later puts you in the Midnight watch, around 10:00 pm and this will be the approximate time of the conditional rapture of Jewish believers. 3 ½ years after that (2:00 am, Cockcrowing Watch) is Satan's Advent (when the Man of Sin stands in the Holy Place, is assassinated, and rises from the dead), and then 3 ½ years after that is the end of the Morning watch (6:00am) when the Lord Jesus Christ will return to the Earth (2nd Advent)!!!

CHART 9

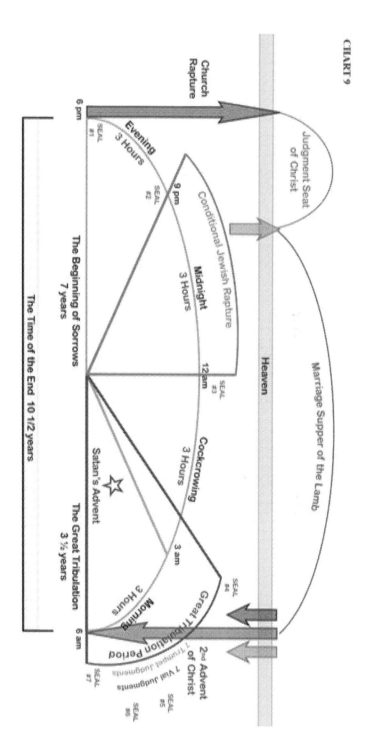

137

If the conditional rapture is at 10 pm according to God's prophetic time clock, and we are aware of the prophetic "hour" of Christ's sudden knock at the door, bear in mind that the 60 prophetic minutes contained in the 10 pm hour is the earthly equivalent of 316 days![274] 316 days to watch and pray is a lot better than 3.42 YEARS (the length of the entire Midnight watch of 1,231 days), but still, as you can see, Christ's statement of no one knowing the day or the hour is still correct because no one will be able to know the EXACT LITERAL DAY OR HOUR of this conditional rapture.

There is no way around it: the Jews MUST **"watch and pray"** that they may **"be accounted worthy to ESCAPE all these things that shall come to pass, and to STAND before the Son of man"**[275] in heaven at the Marriage Supper of the Lamb.

---

[274] Here's the math:

1.14 hrs/1 yr x 60 min/1 hr = 68.4 min/1 yr

68.4 min/1 yr divided by 1 yr/360 days = .19 min / 1 day

60 min/1 hr divided by .19 min / 1 day = **315.79 days/1 hr**

  The 60 minutes in the 10:00 hour is the prophetic equivalent of 316 days.

[275] **Luke 21:36**

CHAPTER 15

The Year of the Rapture of the Church

    This is a secret 'bonus' chapter, and serves as a 'reward' for those who read this entire thesis. This chapter is not listed in the table of contents for the simple reason that most readers would skip to the end to see what kind of "date setting" was taking place, and would be thoroughly confused by the timeframes and prophetic measurements used to determine this date of the rapture of the Church. Nevertheless, now that there is ample evidence to support a 10 ½ year long Time of the End, it is theoretically possible to know the approximate year of our Bridegroom's return.

    As far as we Christians know, the SPECIFIC DATE of Christ's return for the Church is not directly given in the Bible. Many would say that this is because *"Jesus said that no man can know the day or the hour"*, but as it has already been pointed out, that verse (**Matthew 24:36, Mark 13:32**) has absolutely NOTHING to do with the rapture of the CHURCH, and trying to insert the Body of Christ into Matthew 24 (which contextually is dealing with the Tribulation and the 2nd Advent) is about the most obscene form of Bible interpretation that one could ever conjecture.

    The specific date of the rapture of the Church is not given, however I believe another date is: the date of the start of the Millennium. This date is hidden in **Hosea 5:15 - 6:2:**

5:15 I will go *and* return to my place, till they acknowledge their offence, and seek my face: in their affliction they will seek me early.

6:1 Come, and let us return unto the LORD: for he hath torn, and he will heal us; he hath smitten, and he will bind us up.

v.2 After TWO DAYS will he revive us: in the THIRD DAY he will raise us up, and we shall live in his sight.

    The person speaking in the passage is obviously none other than the Lord Himself. The 'going' and 'returning' to 'his place' is a reference to His 1st Advent: He left His "place" (Heaven: **Matthew 1:25**) and returned in AD 33 (the ascension: **Acts 1:9**) and will remain in Heaven and will not return to the earth until

"they acknowledge their offence". The reference is to the Jewish people and the offence is their rejection of their Messiah (**John 19:15, Matthew 27:25**). The Great Tribulation period is the **"affliction"** that will cause the Jewish people, after nearly 2,000 years, to finally begin to seek the face of God again. The sentiment of the Jewish people at that time will be **"Come, and let us return unto the LORD: for he hath torn, and he will heal us; he hath smitten, and he will bind us up."** This is an acknowledgement that they have sinned against God and that the awful suffering they have been going through for the last 3 ½ years was from God and justly deserved. They, like the prophet Jeremiah, will lament: **"The LORD is righteous; for I have rebelled against his commandment"**[276]. The prophet Micah rehearsed the repentant words that the nation of Israel will someday speak when he said **"I will bear the indignation of the LORD, <u>because I have sinned against him</u>, until he plead my cause, and execute judgment for me: he will bring me forth to the light, *and* I shall behold his righteousness."**[277]

The statement in Hosea continues and there is an assertion that **"after two days will he revive us"**. Perhaps the nation of Israel will repent 48 hours (two literal days) before the 2nd Advent, but it is more likely that the **"days"** here are two prophetic days that are the equivalent of 2,000 years, as revealed in **2 Peter 3:8**[278].

The first important thing to pay attention to is <u>when</u> the **"two days"** begin: the two days are either AFTER the offence or AFTER the Lord's ascension, but either way, we are to begin the 2,000 year countdown from AD 33 (assuming the historical calendar is accurate, and not off by 4 years).

The second important thing to pay attention to is the fact that the great event after the culmination of those 2,000 years is NOT the rapture of the Church! There is no rapture anywhere in the passage and there are no born again Gentile believers anywhere in the passage! The 'reviving' in **Hosea 6:2** is exclusive to the JEWISH people; the 'reviving' is NOT the bodily ascension of individuals

---

[276] **Lamentations 1:18**

[277] **Micah 7:9**

[278] **2 Peter 3:8** But, beloved, be not ignorant of this one thing, that <u>one day *is* with the Lord as a thousand years, and a thousand years as one day.</u>

140

into Heaven, it is the resurrection and restoration of an entire nation[279] which occurs after the battle of Armageddon and at the start of the Millennium! Now add up the numbers:

AD 33 (the offence of the Jews / ascension of Jesus Christ)
+ 2,000 years (two prophetic days)
AD 2033

September, during the Feast of Tabernacles **AD 2033**, would be **the date of the 2nd Advent and start of the Millennium.** If this date is accurate, we can theoretically ascertain the date of the rapture by subtracting the number of years of the Time of the End.
If the Time of the End was 7 years long, then the rapture of the Church would be in AD 2026 (2033 – 7 years = 2026). …but the Time of the End is not 7 years long.

If the Time of the End was roughly 4 years long, then the rapture of the Church would be in AD 2029 (2033 – 4 years = 2029). …but the Time of the End is not roughly 4 years long.

IF this thesis is correct, and the Time of the End is exactly 10 ½ years long; and IF the **"two days"** in **Hosea 6:2** is exactly 2,000 years; and IF our calendar accurate and is not 4 years off, then MY OPINION is that **the rapture of the Church will occur in the spring of AD 2023**.

Not much time left. Are you ready?

Even so, come Lord Jesus.

_____

[279] Ezekiel 37:11 Then he said unto me, Son of man, these bones are the whole house of Israel: behold, they say, Our bones are dried, and our hope is lost: we are cut off for our parts.
v.12 Therefore prophesy and say unto them, Thus saith the Lord GOD; Behold, O my people, I will open your graves, and cause you to come up out of your graves, and bring you into the land of Israel.
v.13 And ye shall know that I *am* the LORD, when I have opened your graves, O my people, and brought you up out of your graves,
v.14 And shall put my spirit in you, and ye shall live, and I shall place you in your own land: then shall ye know that I the LORD have spoken *it*, and performed *it*, saith the LORD.

CHART 9

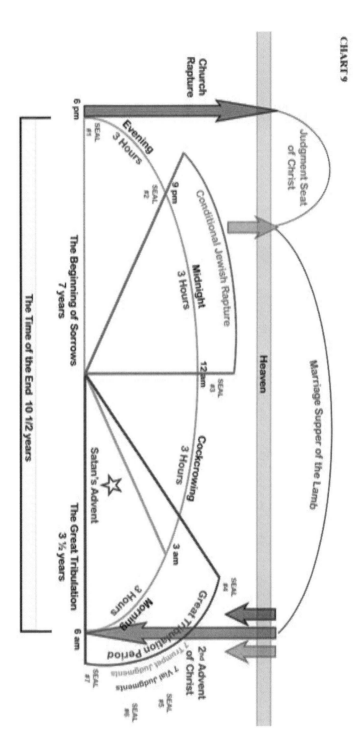

144

Printed in Great Britain
by Amazon

59480243R00090